ON STRENGTH

ON STRENGTH

A Philosophical Dialogue

Nicholas J. Pappas

Algora Publishing
New York

Library of Congress Cataloging-in-Publication Data —

Pappas, Nicholas J.
  Strength / Nicholas J. Pappas.
    p. cm.
  Includes bibliographical references and index.
    ISBN 978-0-87586-939-1 (pbk.: alk. paper) — ISBN 978-0-87586-940-7 (alk. paper)
— ISBN 978-0-87586-941-4 (ebook)
    1. Self-confidence—Miscellanea. 2. Success—Miscellanea. 3. Conduct of life—
Miscellanea. I. Title.
    BJ1533.S27P37 2012
    179'.9—dc23
                2012033441

Front cover: © Michael Kloth/Corbis

Printed in the United States

To Theodora Pappas

INTRODUCTION

On Strength is the story of Youth. He has many strengths. But he also has vulnerabilities. Director and Father explore a variety of topics with him in hopes of encouraging him to tap his strengths and overcome his weaknesses.

The dialogue is in large part about building confidence, but doing so without crossing the line to overconfidence.

The characters discuss heart, mind, gut, and soul. But most importantly they talk about truth, truth in the broadest sense. Youth goes so far as to declare that truth can make you whole.

Director often probes and qualifies the statements of the other two characters. But he is not without limitations of his own. There are times when he might be expected to speak, or to say something in particular, but doesn't. This gives some sense of the limits under which he operates.

Father seems to have the opposite problem, in that he occasionally speaks when one might think he should leave it to the others. But despite any shortcomings, his virtues should be clear. And his love for his son is obvious.

Nick Pappas

On Strength

Director

Father

Youth

1

Youth: And then he punched me in the nose.

Director: What happened next?

Youth: I tripped and fell. Then everybody laughed.

Father: And that is why it's time to hit the weights and learn some martial arts. You've got to build your strength and learn to fight.

Director: An excellent idea. The weights will train the body while the martial arts will train the mind.

Youth: But martial arts are all about the body, too. Your mind can't throw a punch.

Director: Of course. But martial artists worth their salt have knowledge and a fair amount of discipline.

Father: Director's right. The body must obey the mind.

Youth: And what does mind obey?

Father: The character.

Director: Now tell us, Youth. Are you aware of what your character consists?

Youth: It's what you value.

Director: You must hold those values, right?

Youth: That's right.

Director: Can you imagine fighting for those values?

Youth: Yes.

Director: What's worse? To lose your values or to lose a fight with fists?

Youth: To lose your values, certainly.

Director: This battle for your character, what strength does it require?

Youth: The strength of holding on, of never letting go.

Director: And what about a value that is bad?

Youth: I'd never hold a value that is bad.

Director: Alright. But let me ask you this. Do you believe it's possible a value that you thought was good is really bad?

Youth: Well, I suppose it's possible. But I would drop a value that I learned was bad.

Director: Let's check this with your father now. Do you agree that Youth should drop such values?

Father: Yes. You have to drop these values right away, my boy, as soon as it is clear they're bad — no matter how it makes you feel. You're going to find all sorts of values in this world. And some of those that are not good might take you in.

Youth: Some boys at school have values that are bad. And they're the ones who pick on me.

Director: They pick on you because of what you hold, because of what you think?

Youth: They do.

Director: Just what do they believe in, Youth?

Youth: I guess it's not so much what they believe. It's what they don't.

Director: Can you describe what they do not believe?

Youth: They don't think they should be polite. They don't believe in being nice.

Director: Do you believe that they are strong?

Youth: They're stronger with their fists.

Director: If you were stronger with your fists, would it be easier to hold on tight to what you think is right?

Youth: I think it would.

Director: So character and fists are complementary?

Youth: They are.

Director: Until you've learned to fight, do you believe it's possible these boys will beat the character right out of you? Or can you hold on tight despite their worst?

Youth: Of course I can hold on.

Director: What makes it so you can?

Youth: My will.

Director: Just what exactly is the will?

Youth: It's holding on again. It's holding on to what you want.

Director: And that is what, for you?

Youth: Besides a solid character? I want to learn to fight.

Director: And so you'll will yourself to learn?

Youth: That's right.

Director: You'll will yourself to make your body strong?

Youth: I will.

Director: And what about your mind?

Youth: The will is in the mind.

Director: But doesn't mind consist of parts?

Youth: What parts?

Director: There's will, and then there is the part that thinks. Or don't you think you have to think?

Youth: Of course you have to think. That's how you know the things you want.

Director: And so there's thought then will? Should thought be strong, or only will?

Youth: I think it should be strong.

Director: And what does strong thought mean?

Youth: It means you think your way through difficult terrain.

Director: Terrain? You mean like deserts, mountains, and the like?

Youth: Of course — as metaphors.

Director: But metaphors for what?

Youth: For anything that's difficult.

Director: Like knowing whether you should just surrender to the boys who pick on you?

Youth: That isn't very difficult.

Director: You didn't have to think to know you wouldn't just give up?

Youth: Of course I didn't have to think.

Director: Then what was it that told you what to do?

Youth: My character?

Director: But don't you have to know your character is good, is worth defending?

Youth: Yes.

Director: What tells you if your character is good?

Youth: It must be thought.

Director: You think about the values that you hold, the values that make up your character? I mean, you don't just take them as mere articles of faith?

Youth: I think about the values, yes. You have to have good reasons for the values that you hold.

Director: What reasons have you got?

Youth: It isn't easy to explain.

Director: But do your reasons all amount to this? The values that you hold will make you happy in the end?

Youth: They do amount to that.

Director: And are you happy now?

Youth: You mean aside from being beaten up? I'd say I am.

Director: But you're not sure?

Youth: I'm not sure that I'm happy yet. But often times I'm proud.

Director: Do you believe that pride can be the basis for your happiness?

Youth: I'd like to think it can.

Director: And what's the basis for your pride?

Youth: My strength in holding on to all my values, right?

Director: And so we have a pyramid? The base is in your strength, atop of which is pride, atop of which sits happiness?

Youth: That sounds alright to me.

Director: But is there something more?

Youth: Like what?

Director: Like pleasure, Youth. Or don't you think that pleasure follows from your happiness?

Youth: But I'm not sure that pleasure ought to be the highest thing.

Director: Should it be happiness? And then should pleasure be the thing it rests upon?

Youth: I don't like how that sounds. I think it's better if your pride supports your happiness.

Director: Well, maybe pleasure is the lowest thing?

Youth: No, strength must be the base.

Director: Then maybe pleasure sits directly on that base?

Youth: Then pride is pushed away from strength. That doesn't make much sense.

Director: Should we remove all pleasure from our pyramid?

Youth: I think that might be best. With strength, and pride, and happiness I think we have enough.

Director: Then there's no pleasure in the life we live?

Youth: Of course there is. It's just a separate thing. I mean, you could be weak, and full of shame, and not the least bit happy, yet it's possible for you to feel a pleasure simply lying in the sun.

Director: Now tell us, Father, what you make of this.

Father: Well, I believe, essentially, that happiness and pleasure are as one. I think the person in the sun is happy for a brief amount of time, however fleetingly.

Youth: But what of values then? Don't you believe that holding them, and only holding them, will bring you happiness? It takes no values to feel pleasure in the sun.

Father: But we, my boy, would have a happiness and pleasure that will last. The ground for that is in your character. The values that you hold will guide you toward a pleasure, pride, and happiness that will endure.

Director: But that is only if your character is good? I mean, an evil man can't find the way to happiness. Or do you disagree?

Youth: Well, that's the thing. An evil man feels pleasure in his wicked deeds. But he will never feel the least amount of happiness. That's proof that happiness and pleasure aren't the same. Or do we say the pleasure of an evil act is good, that it brings happiness?

Director: I don't see how we can. But tell me, Youth. Can evil men be proud of evil acts?

Youth: I think they can, and often are — at least as far as I can see from how it is at school. The bullies all seem proud of how they act.

Director: And yet they're miserable inside?

Youth: I think they are.

Director: Is that because they put their strength to evil use?

Youth: It is.

Director: And what exactly is an evil use? Is it just anything that makes you miserable?

Youth: I guess.

Director: Do you believe the Devil must be miserable, assuming he is real?

Youth: I think he must.

Director: And you know this because you know what evil is, and he is it?

Youth: I do. And yes, he is.

Director: And how do you know this?

Youth: You're asking how I know my right from wrong? Well, I just know.

Director: Do you believe the Devil knows?

Youth: Of course he knows.

Director: Does everybody know?

Youth: I think they do, unless they've lost their minds, or else they're very young.

Director: How old are we when we begin to know?

Youth: I'd say we know the basics by the time we're ten.

Director: The basics are enough to last you all your life?

Youth: The basics are the same no matter what.

Director: The thorniest, most difficult of problems in the world can be resolved by what a ten-year-old should know?

Youth: You make it sound ridiculous. But still, I think the answer's yes.

Director: What are these basics, Youth?

Youth: You shouldn't harm, except in self-defense. You shouldn't lie. You shouldn't steal. Etcetera.

Director: You mentioned one exception here — you shouldn't harm except in self-defense. But what about exceptions for the other two? Or are there none?

Youth: It sometimes seems you have to lie. And maybe there are times when you might have to steal.

Director: You learn about exceptions later on, when you are more than ten?

Youth: That's right.

Director: Perhaps the Devil makes exceptions all the time.

Youth: I think he does.

Director: So he must think he's in the right?

Youth: I think he knows he's in the wrong. That's why he isn't happy.

Director: I'm not sure I understand. He makes exceptions, yes?

Youth: He knows that his exceptions are not truly warranted.

Director: And yet he makes them anyway?

Youth: What can I say? He's the Devil, right?

Director: Well, that's enough of him. So tell me, Youth. Do you believe it takes great strength of character to tell no lies?

Youth: I do.

Director: Does it take strength in order not to steal?

Youth: For me it doesn't, no.

Director: Why not?

Youth: I don't need anything. And I don't want to break the law.

Director: And what about committing harm? Does it take strength to stop yourself from doing that?

Youth: I guess if I were really mad it would.

Director: Is that the reason that a man might work a harm, because he's mad? Or would he sometimes do it in cold blood?

Youth: I think he often does it in cold blood.

Director: And what's the reason for this act?

Youth: I think he hates.

Director: Does it take strength to hate?

Youth: No, I don't think it does.

Director: Does it take strength to love?

Youth: It does.

Director: Can you say why?

Youth: You have to stick with someone through both thick and thin.

Director: Do those who fill their souls with hate have love?

Youth: How could they? No.

Director: Is love a part of character?

Youth: It is. You value love. And when you do, you have a loving heart and soul.

Director: And heart and soul are where the strength of character resides? Or is it in the mind?

Youth: It's in all three.

Director: I wonder if you've heard it said that heart, and soul, and mind should be as one.

Youth: I have.

Director: And if they're one, do you believe they're all the same? In other words, could it be said that heart and soul are really just a part of mind?

Youth: You mean to say they don't exist?

Director: Oh no. They do exist, of course. But do you think that heart is really in your beating heart?

Youth: At times it feels it is. But I can see how we might say that heart can be a part of mind. It's possible to think with heart. But soul is soul. It isn't part of mind. If anything, the mind is part of it.

Director: Where does the soul reside?

Youth: It's everywhere. It's who you are.

Director: So soul must be the strongest thing?

Youth: It has to be.

Director: Is soul a sort of whole, while all the other things are parts?

Youth: Exactly, yes.

Director: Do you believe that wholes are greater than the sum of all their parts?

Youth: I do.

Director: What makes a soul grow strong?

Youth: You have to nourish it.

Director: You mean you have to care for all the parts? Or do you simply care for soul?

Youth: You have to care for everything.

Director: With love?

Youth: Of course.

Director: Would this be love and care from you, or love and care from someone else?

Youth: How could a soul grow strong from someone else's love and care?

Director: I think there's someone here who has a word or two to say on that.

Father: You're right. I do. A child's soul can be quite strong all on its own. But it takes nurturing to make it strong for good, and not for ill. That's where your character comes in. A parent helps to form the character. And character will reinforce the native strength of soul.

Youth: But character is only part of soul.

Father: However that may be, it is a crucial part. The values of the character are capable of steering your whole soul.

Youth: But what about the heart and mind? I mean, can't these two turn a value out if it seems bad, just as they're capable of taking a new value in? So what is steering what?

Father: You're right to ask, my boy. The answer? You. You steer yourself, once you are old enough. And how do you do this? Is it by means of character or heart or mind? And what are you that's steered? Your soul? I'll tell you now. You're old enough. These things are merely words. The knowledge that you need to steer goes far beyond mere words. I like to think of it as knowledge in your gut. But that is just a word, as well.

Youth: I like that word. But how do I get knowledge in my gut?

Father: You simply have it, Youth. Your gut is everything you know all wrapped in one. So trust it when it speaks.

2

Director: Your gut is everything you know? I thought that gut is what you feel.

Father: It is. But what you feel derives from what you know.

Director: And what you know derives from what you think?

Father: Not always so, but often, yes.

Director: And what about beliefs? Aren't they a part of gut?

Father: They are.

Director: Beliefs can come from thoughts?

Father: They can.

Director: So where is strength in all of this?

Father: You must be strong to think, believe, and know.

Director: I see. We said you think your way through difficult terrain. The landscape of belief can be the same and worse?

Father: It can. You have to keep believing through both thick and thin.

Director: That sounds like what we said of love.

Father: All love is rooted in belief.

Director: Belief in what?

Father: Belief in what the other is.

Director: Why, can't you know just what the other is, and not believe?

Father: I think we're splitting hairs.

Director: You think belief and knowledge are the same?

Father: Of course I don't — not strictly speaking, no. But things get complicated. I know you're an honest man. And I believe that you're an honest man. What difference is there here?

Director: When you believe you do not know. And when you know you don't believe. The difference has to do with facts. Belief is short on facts. Or isn't that the way it works?

Father: If that's the way it is, then I can never know that you're an honest man. It's impossible for me to gather all the facts. I'd have to talk to everyone you've ever known to see if you had always told the truth. And even then, you might have lied to all of them with skill and never been found out. Or should I simply base my judgment on the facts I know firsthand? That's why we say that I know you to be an honest man, the emphasis on "I." In my experience you're an honest man. But I don't know the rest. So I believe, and know, that you're an honest man. How's that?

Director: If you believe in someone's honesty, what makes it hard to carry on in that belief? Is it just hard when there is evidence that shakes your faith? Is that when you need strength in your belief, to go against the facts?

Father: Well, that's not faith. That's foolishness.

Director: And so you weigh the evidence and then decide what you'll believe?

Father: Of course.

Director: Then when is strength required for our belief?

Father: You need it when you think the evidence against what you believe is weak, but others think it's strong.

Director: And what's the opposite?

Father: The opposite? It's thinking that the evidence against what you believe is strong, while others think it's weak, I guess.

Director: And if the evidence against what you believe is strong, what should you do?

Father: Well, you should stop believing, then.

Director: You've heard of wishful thinking, Youth?

Youth: I have.

Director: Do you know what it is?

Youth: When you believe against the evidence.

Director: And what's the opposite?

Youth: When you believe along with all the evidence.

Director: Despite the fact the crowd might think things otherwise?

Youth: Despite the fact. I've done this sort of thing before at school, you know. The crowd accused a friend of mine of telling lies. But on the evidence I felt it wasn't true. I took a stand with him and he was vindicated in the end.

Director: You ought to feel some pride for what you did.

Youth: I do.

Director: But what if you were wrong? Suppose your friend was really telling lies, and you found out.

Youth: Then I could not stick up for him like that.

Director: Some people say, you know, it doesn't matter if your friend is right or wrong — you must stick up for him the same.

Youth: But shouldn't you stick up for truth?

Director: The truth is more important than your loyalty?

Youth: My loyalty is based on truth, on truth that's shared. If it were any other way we'd merely have the loyalty of thieves.

Director: That's fine, my friend. But loyalty like this, it seems to me, will take a great reserve of strength.

Youth: Because the truth is difficult?

Director: It often seems it is. Don't you agree?

Youth: I do. I'd like to build my strength so I can handle great amounts of truth.

Director: And how will you do that?

Youth: I'll start with simple truths and work my way from there.

Father: But simple truths are often hard.

Youth: Then where should I begin?

Director: Begin with what's before you, Youth.

Youth: And how do I begin?

Father: You take a bite and chew until you get the flavor of the truth.

Youth: And then I have to swallow it?

Father: Of course. And then you must digest the truth. And when you have, you know it well.

Director: Do you believe the well digested food of truth will make us strong?

Father: What better nourishment for strength?

Director: But that is only if we really have the truth.

Father: Of course.

Director: So how can we be sure of what we have?

Father: I think it all comes down to gut.

Director: You mean that if a thing you ate has made you sick right in your gut, you know it can't be true?

Father: I can't see how it could be true.

Director: Well, maybe you forgot to chew. And maybe you forgot to eat in moderation, too.

Youth: Suppose you chewed and ate a moderate amount.

Father: Then yes, that's how it works — it can't be true if it has made you sick. You have to learn to trust your gut concerning truth.

Youth: But what if I eat truth and feel just fine, but someone else takes in the same, and chews and doesn't have too much, and he feels sick?

Father: That truth is not for him.

Youth: But isn't truth for everyone?

Father: In different times of life, I think it's possible that's true. A truth for you might not be one for someone younger, right?

Youth: I guess.

Director: And what about the ones they say are wise beyond their years?

Father: They stomach truths before their peers.

Director: Then let us hope that they digest them properly, and don't just learn to live with feeling sick.

Youth: Would it take strength to live with feeling sick?

Director: I think it would. But it would sap that strength. Imagine that you ate some truths for older men, and you felt sick but carried on. What strength would you have left for other truths, the truths becoming to your age?

Youth: Do you believe that being wise beyond your years is good?

Director: Well, I believe it's what you make of it. But there is one important thing I'd add.

Youth: What's that?

Director: There is no shame in throwing something up.

Youth: But that would mean you're weak.

Director: You'd rather you continued to feel sick? Suppose you had an allergy to certain foods, an allergy that makes you spew the food back out. Do you believe there's shame in that?

Youth: You mean there's nothing I can do? My body just reacts, despite whatever strength I have? I guess that there's no shame. It can't be helped.

Director: But if it could be helped, if there were something you could do, you'd think there's shame?

Youth: I would.

Director: Then let me ask you this. Can everybody help it when it comes to moral truths?

Youth: You mean, can everyone have moral strength? I think they can.

Director: So there is always shame for those who weaken here?

Youth: There is. We all are equal here.

Director: A man who lies is weak?

Youth: He is.

Director: A man who steals is weak?

Youth: He is.

Director: A man who harms another man is weak?

Youth: I'd like to say he is.

Director: What holds you back? Is it because he's strong enough to harm, yet weak enough to harm?

Youth: Exactly that.

Director: We'd say his moral code is weak? But what is strong?

Youth: His body is what's strong.

Director: Alright. But aren't there other cases, too? What other kinds of strength are there?

Youth: There's strength of will. That might be how he works his harm.

Director: You mean, for instance, he might will himself to harm another man, and wills this over time, with many little, wicked, willful acts along the way?

Youth: Exactly, yes.

Director: But there is nothing wrong, per se, with strength of will, correct?

Youth: That's true. But strength of will is only good when harnessed to a proper end.

Director: Now, is there shame in will that's used improperly?

Youth: There ought to be.

Director: What's worse? Strong will toward evil ends or very little strength of will, or none at all, toward good? To which should shame attach?

Youth: To both.

Director: But which is worse?

Youth: To serve an evil end.

Director: And why is that?

Youth: Because an evil end works harm.

Father: And lack of strength, my boy, can work no harm? Does it take strength to stand up for the truth?

Youth: Of course it does.

Father: If you're a witness to a crime and you don't have the will to testify, do you work harm?

Youth: You let a criminal go free.

Father: Is that a harm?

Youth: I'd say it is, but in a different sort of way.

Father: Then weakness can give rise to harm, if only in a different way.

Director: So it would seem that you were right to say that shame attaches both to strength of will in evil or in simple weakness of the will toward good.

Youth: That's why we have to exercise our wills — but exercise them toward the good.

Director: The good we simply know from when we're ten?

Youth: Agreed.

Father: But what if how we see the good is complicated by some things we learn in later years?

Youth: But good is simple, isn't it?

Father: Not always, Youth. At times it even seems it's contradictory.

Youth: So what are we to do?

Father: We exercise our wills toward the good we know. And if the way we see this good should change, then we must change as well. It's very hard to learn that something that you thought was good is not.

Youth: Well, maybe we should wait to exercise our wills until we know, we know for sure, that we are aiming at the good.

Father: The problem is it always seems for sure.

Youth: You mean there is no way to know? We're just engaged in empty exercise of will?

Father: If you believe you're serving good, there is no emptiness.

Youth: But we should know we're serving good, not just believe.

Father: Sometimes belief is all you've got.

Director: And that's because the good you held and what you've learned seem contradictory? In other words, the thing you thought you knew was good appears in this new light to be much less than simply good? And so you always have some doubts and therefore must believe, not know, concerning any good you come to see from here on out?

Father: That's right.

Youth: But maybe there's a way to reconcile the old and new so both are good.

Father: If only that were so.

Director: Suppose you were to spoil a child. It seems a good idea at first. But later, when it's much too late, you learn it was a bad mistake.

Father: You have to catch mistakes in time.

Director: And how do you do that?

Father: As soon as there's a sign that something's wrong, you have to make a change. You cannot wait.

Director: And why do you think people wait?

Father: I think they're weak.

Director: It takes much strength to know the signs and act on them?

Father: I think it takes a great amount of strength.

Director: And why is that?

Father: The signs don't come immediately. They only come in time. By then you're settled in your ways. Inertia can be very hard to overcome.

Director: Agreed. Now, spoiling is when you're too soft. The antidote is being firm. Correct?

Father: Correct.

Director: The problem isn't being soft, per se. The problem is you're never firm.

Father: That's right. You're never strong.

Director: But don't you think that being soft requires strength?

Father: You mean the strength of holding back, the strength of gentleness? I do.

Director: You need to know what sort of strength to bring to bear and when. And in this way the opposites are reconciled, the opposites of firm and soft.

Does that make sense?

Father: It does.

Director: Can you see how a parent who has been too soft might come to think that gentleness is simply bad?

Father: I can. And that's a bad mistake. This person needs the antidote — the antidote in time, before it is too late.

Director: The antidote can save the good?

Father: It can.

Director: And if you have the antidote, if you know what to do, what if you lack the strength to make the change?

Father: You mean you know, you really know, exactly what to do?

Director: Do you believe it's possible to know like that?

Father: I think it's rare, but yes. So let me answer you. With knowledge of the thing to do you always have the strength — or rather, you can always find the strength — to make the change.

Director: You don't believe it's possible to know but lack the means to put your knowledge into use?

Father: No, I have faith in what I know — in what I truly know. If you are strong enough to know, then you are strong enough to do.

Director: This has the force of law with you?

Father: It does.

Director: But what if, for example, you're aware that someone else's child is being spoiled? Do you step in and act? Or do you leave things well enough alone?

Father: I think we ought to try to help.

Director: What can we do?

Father: We let the parents know we think that something's wrong — but tactfully.

Director: Suppose that they ignore our words. What then?

Father: We try to set the child straight ourselves.

Director: That's rather bold. What do we do?

Father: We're firm.

Director: And if the child retreats from us, what then?

Father: Then I suppose there's little we can do. We have to let him go. And that's a shame.

Youth: But still, we tried. That counts for something, right?

Director: It does, most certainly. Now, our law applies to many sorts of things, and not just spoiled brats. And I suppose in all but every case there is a line that we won't cross.

Youth: What sort of line?

Director: A line that says, for instance, just how far we'll go in being firm to someone else's child. Now, is a line like this a sign of strength, or does it show how weak we really are?

Youth: I think it shows our strength. We could have crossed the line quite easily but stopped.

Director: And so we act as far as our knowledge goes, until we hit a line? Is that the way to formulate the law?

Youth: It is. But we should be the ones to say where there's a line.

Director: Does it take strength to draw the line?

Youth: I think it does.

Director: And would we draw from strength if we draw randomly?

Youth: Of course we wouldn't, no.

Director: Does it seem best to draw from knowledge, then?

Youth: It does.

Director: And what's our knowledge of?

Youth: Of what's appropriate.

Director: Just how are we to know exactly what's appropriate?

Youth: I think it's hard to know. I think at first we have to guess.

Director: You mean we must experiment?

Youth: Exactly, yes.

Director: And what if in the course of our experiments we learn that there are other lines?

Father: I'm sure we will. The world is full of lines.

Youth: But are these lines from knowledge, Dad?

Father: No, most of them are not.

Director: Can we ignore the ones that aren't?

Father: How can we, friend? They are supported by brute force.

Director: And that's the only way they'll hold?

Father: Of course.

Youth: Whenever lines aren't from experiments or reasoned arguments they always need brute force.

Director: So if we draw a line from all the certainty we gain from our experiments and arguments we won't need force to back it up?

Youth: That's right. The strength of truth will back it up.

3

Director: This strength of truth, can we suppose it's like a wave?

Youth: Why not?

Director: Do you believe it's possible to surf this wave?

Youth: To surf a wave of truth? What would that mean?

Director: Why, we'd just paddle out, then wait, then catch our wave, and ride it in.

Youth: But ride it in to where?

Director: The shore, of course — unless we just go right back out again to catch another wave.

Youth: And what's the shore?

Director: The shore is pride and happiness. Or don't you think the strength of truth brings that?

Father: I'll tell you what brings that — the lines that we've been speaking of. They're how we rule ourselves. And if we rule ourselves the way we should, we will feel pride and happiness.

Director: Self-rule can make us stronger than we were before we had our lines?

Father: It can. It helps us concentrate our strength.

Youth: Then how come there are those without a set of lines who seem quite strong?

Father: They have their lines. But they are hidden from our view.

Youth: Then how can you be sure they have their lines?

Father: If strength is water, it is water that you must contain. The lines you draw create containers for your strength. Without these lines your strength is poured out uselessly, as though on sand.

Youth: So all of us need lines. But should we hide those lines or make them clear to everyone?

Director: What benefit is there to hiding them?

Youth: You don't let on how far you'll go.

Director: Because you'll go quite far?

Youth: Or maybe you won't go that far at all.

Director: But can't we simply watch and see exactly where a person stops and then we'll know the way he draws his lines?

Youth: But what if someone fakes? Suppose he acts as though his line were here, but no, it's really there.

Director: He'd have to put on quite an act. But still, you're right. That's possible.

Father: Regardless of what's possible, I think it's best to be upfront about your lines. Misunderstandings can arise about a hidden line. And it takes strength to sort them out.

Youth: But what if you're upfront and someone wants to push you past your line?

Father: Why, you just push him back.

Youth: Suppose this happens every day for many lines.

Father: Then you'll grow strong from all the pushing that you do.

Youth: Or you'll grow weak because you're all worn out.

Director: How many lines do you believe we have to draw?

Youth: Let's say that there are ten.

Director: Well, with these ten let's say we've got a choice. The lines can be where people draw them usually. Or we can draw them in a way that is uniquely ours.

Youth: So if we draw them as per usual it won't take too much strength in order to defend the lines?

Director: Perhaps. But if we draw them as our own, what then?

Youth: It all depends. Suppose the line in question has to do with lies. A line drawn close would leave us fighting to maintain the truth. A line drawn far would leave us lying up a storm.

Director: Is closer always stricter, Youth?

Youth: That's how it seems to me.

Director: And further out is looser, right? If so, what takes more strength?

Youth: The stricter line, of course.

Director: If that is how it is, would all our lines be drawn in tight?

Youth: I think we'd have to choose. Too many tight might wear us down.

Director: So two are tight, while eight are loose?

Youth: No, I would say that two are tight while eight are at the norm.

Director: And if we were to gain in strength we'd move another in?

Youth: We would — as many as we could.

Director: Because it's best to have our lines drawn tight?

Youth: It is.

Director: But maybe our example has misled us, Youth.

Youth: How so?

Director: We know we do not want to go too far with lies, if we go anywhere at all. But what about with generosity? Should we be strict and tight?

Youth: Of course we shouldn't be. We should be somewhat loose, but not completely so. Our generosity can only go so far before it saps our substance and our strength. We need to know the right amount, not just as much as possible.

Director: Now, where are we most likely to be pushed?

Youth: Tight in, for sure. But bullies also push the people at the norm, and sometimes even those who are far out.

Director: And where's the hardest fight?

Father: If someone's pushing you it's difficult wherever you might draw the line.

Director: So what are we to do?

Youth: We have to push him back.

Director: Indeed. But do you think this is the only use of all our strength? Do we do more than just defend our line?

Youth: You think that we should act offensively?

Director: Suppose we know a man who draws his line of generosity quite tight. He has great wealth but never shares. Would it be good to nudge him past his line?

Youth: I think it would.

Director: And can you think of other cases just like this?

Youth: I can.

Director: It's good to use our strength with them offensively, if that is not too strong a word?

Youth: It is.

Director: How do we separate ourselves from bullies who would do the same?

Youth: A bully doesn't nudge. He pushes very hard.

Director: So we must exercise restraint, and use our strength judiciously.

Youth: Judiciously — exactly that. A bully doesn't act judiciously.

Director: If you would act judiciously you'd have to act from knowledge, yes?

Youth: Agreed.

Director: And bullies lack real knowledge of the thing in question, right?

Youth: That's right.

Father: Could we have found another law? Your knowledge always makes you act judiciously?

Youth: But can't you know yet fail to act judiciously? You have to live up to your knowledge, right? It's not a given thing.

Father: If you have knowledge of a thing — a knowledge that is true — you can't but act judiciously.

Youth: But what if you deny your knowledge, Dad?

Director: Now, Youth, your question makes me wonder. What about the law that we declared before? If you are strong enough to know, then you are strong enough to do. If you deny your knowledge, then you're weak?

Youth: Of course.

Father: Well, look. These things need not be laws. They're just the way I like to look at things.

Director: You like to think that knowledge is enough?

Father: I do.

Director: And yet it's martial arts for Youth.

Father: The knowledge that he'll learn counts most.

Director: But surely he'll need strength of body, too?

Father: Of course he will.

Director: Is this strength knowledge, friend? Or is it something else?

Father: It's something else.

Director: So knowledge by itself is not enough.

Father: Agreed — though knowledge is the key.

Director: Now what about the view that knowledge always makes you act judiciously? Perhaps we ought to say that knowledge makes it possible to act judiciously.

Youth: What else is needed, then?

Director: I think it's confidence.

Youth: But confidence in what? In what you know?

Director: Indeed — and your ability to act on it.

Youth: Is confidence a sort of strength?

Director: I think it is.

Youth: How do you build this strength?

Director: You have to train it, gradually. You take a step, and then another step. And then you stop and rest. And then you step some more, increasing what you do. That's how it goes.

Youth: So it takes strength to live up to the knowledge that we have. What other sorts of strength are there?

Father: Oh, there are many sorts of strengths.

Youth: Financial strength?

Father: That's one.

Youth: Some say that it's the most important one.

Father: In some ways they are right.

Youth: But how can they be right?

Director: What do you think financial strength is all about?

Youth: A confidence in what you have, in what you own.

Director: As good a definition as I've heard.

Youth: That's it? That's all you have to say?

Father: We all need money, Youth. That's how we live. Or do you know another way?

Youth: What other sorts of strength are there? Political?

Father: That is another sort, of course. And there are more. But I believe all strength boils down to just two types — the kind that's ours alone, and that which comes from other people's strength.

Director: Can you say more?

Father: Our body, and our character, and will, and mental confidence are ours alone. Financial strength, and politics, and anything along those lines, depend on other people's strength.

Youth: But how is that? If you earn money, don't you do it on your own?

Father: That's true. But you are paid by someone else. If you gain confidence, nobody gives you that but you.

Youth: But someone can encourage you, as you've encouraged me.

Father: But in the end you have to take that step of confidence alone, no matter the encouragement you get.

Youth: You said that politics depends on other people's strength. How so? Do you mean votes?

Father: I do. But there is more than votes for office, Youth. You'll find that politics is everywhere. You have to win political support for many things in life.

Youth: I know. We have a sort of politics at school. It has to do with what you think. If you believe what everybody else believes, you're strong politically. But in a better way, you're stronger to believe what no one else believes, because you have to fight the pressure of the crowd.

Director: Suppose that you believe what no one else believes. How do you know that your belief is true? Do you experiment?

Youth: You have to, yes.

Director: Now here's the funny thing. If your experiment can prove the truth of what you think, then why not demonstrate this truth to everyone? Why, you'd be very strong politically.

Youth: Not everyone is open to the truth.

Director: Why not?

Youth: I don't think they are strong enough.

Director: What happens if you try to show the truth to them?

Youth: They get upset with you.

Director: They get upset because they're weak? I thought that they were strong, politically.

Youth: They are. But they're not strong as individuals. That's why they get upset.

Director: Can anyone turn crowds to individuals?

Youth: I don't believe it's possible, unless you separate a person from the crowd and work with him alone, and keep on doing this until there's no more crowd.

Director: Will everybody separate that easily?

Youth: Oh no. They'll often fight you tooth and nail.

Director: Suppose you win that fight. The crowd's no more. But do you know what I am wondering?

Youth: I think I do. Will they stay separated? Won't they form another crowd?

Director: What do you think?

Youth: I think they'll form a crowd.

Director: Can truth exist in crowds?

Youth: I think it can. But it's at risk.

Director: At risk of what?

Youth: Of being changed to something else, to something false.

Director: And why is that?

Youth: The truth must be maintained. You have to live by it. And that takes strength.

Director: Not all the crowd will have this strength?

Youth: To say the least.

Director: But maybe they need shepherding. Are you the one for that?

Youth: Am I? No way. I don't think shepherding is any good.

Director: Because you don't like politics?

Youth: That's right. An individual must tend to his own truths. It's possible to get some help, but you must take this help and run with it alone, not stand in line for shepherding.

Director: Are politicians always shepherds?

Youth: Yes. They're always tending to their flocks.

Director: But can't a politician help an individual?

Youth: I don't see how.

Director: Suppose that his career consists of keeping crowds away from individuals, of getting them to leave the individuals alone.

Youth: But who would vote for him?

Director: Are you assuming there are fewer individuals than members of the crowd?

Youth: But isn't that the way it always is?

Director: I'm not so sure. What makes an individual an individual?

Youth: He's strong all on his own.

Father: There aren't too many people with such strength.

Director: Then, Father, who would vote for him, our politician loyal to the individual, if such a one exists?

Father: Why, only individuals — unless he fools the crowd. He'd have to make them think he's looking out for them.

Director: But he would have to have results along those lines, or else they wouldn't vote him in again.

Father: Perhaps he only gets one term.

Youth: But wait a minute, here. Our politician is a hypocrite? I don't believe that hypocrites will stand up for the truth.

Director: Is that what individuals are all about, the truth?

Youth: Why, yes.

Director: Do you believe it's possible for individuals to form themselves into a crowd?

Youth: Of course, but if they do, they're no longer individuals.

Director: So individuals and those belonging to the crowd are totally opposed?

Youth: They are.

Director: Now crowds have leaders, right?

Youth: Of course.

Director: Do individuals?

Youth: What sort of leaders would they have?

Director: The sort that stand out from the rest. Let's call them naturals.

Youth: How would they lead?

Director: By their example, and by reasoned argument.

Youth: They wouldn't try to herd the people that they lead?

Director: Oh no. They would approach each individual alone, and leave him well enough alone when they had talked.

Father: The problem here is obvious. It isn't possible to talk to everyone.

Director: That's true enough.

Youth: So what about the rest?

Director: Perhaps there will be other naturals who'll work with them.

Youth: And so the politics of naturals is limited in scope to what an individual can do when dealing one-on-one?

Director: It seems that's best. Do you agree?

Youth: I do. But what if certain people take more time to deal with than the rest? What if they drain the naturals?

Director: Are you forgetting that the individuals are strong?

Youth: While that is true in general terms, the needy ones are not.

Director: That isn't always so, my friend. At times there's something sapping strength from someone who is very strong, which makes him seem a needy one. The natural will try to free this person up so he, the one he helps, can use his strength for good.

Youth: But what is good?

Director: I think we ought to ask your father here.

Father: The healthy is the good.

Director: And that's free exercise of strength?

Youth: That can't be it. Free exercise might be toward evil ends.

Director: We need our lines, it seems.

Youth: That's it! The healthy is the exercise of strength within your lines, assuming they are drawn from truth.

Director: In such a case, the stronger that you are the healthier you'll be?

Youth: As long as you can exercise your strength, I think that's true.

Director: What stops the exercise of strength?

Youth: The crowd. It might not think your lines are true.

Director: Is that because it has another truth that contradicts your truth? In other words, there is the truth belonging to the individual and then there is the truth belonging to the crowd?

Youth: I'm not so sure they both are truths. The "truth" belonging to the crowd is often false.

Director: If that's the case, then how do you determine if the crowd is right or wrong?

Youth: You have to use you mind. You have to think.

Director: By means of reasoned argument and bold experiments?

Youth: Exactly so.

Director: How do you know that your conclusions are the truth?

Youth: You check them many times.

Director: Do you consult with other individuals?

Youth: You do.

Director: But if no individuals are there, what do you do?

Youth: You have to trust yourself and act accordingly.

Director: And if it soon appears that you were wrong?

Youth: You make adjustments and you try again.

Director: Does it take strength in order to correct your wrong?

Youth: It does. And that's the reason many people don't correct themselves.

Director: Suppose they have the strength. Why wouldn't they correct their wrongs?

Youth: Their conscience might not bother them.

Director: What is the conscience, Youth?

Youth: I think it's made up of the lines we draw.

Director: Suppose our lines are false. What happens then?

Youth: Our conscience doesn't bother us?

Director: You mean it wouldn't bother you if you drew lines way off the mark?

Youth: Well, it would bother me.

Director: Then why not someone else?

Youth: Because I'm sensitive to things like this.

Director: You're sensitive to truth?

Youth: I am.

Director: But isn't everyone?

Youth: To some degree. But not like us.

4

Director: Are you aware that there are those who say that sensitivity's a sign of weakness, Youth?

Youth: I am.

Director: What do you say to that?

Youth: I say that when you're sensitive you have to use a great amount of strength to bring yourself in line with truth. You sense more truth than those who are insensitive. And so you have a lot more work to do.

Director: Does this seem fair to you?

Youth: At times it doesn't, no. At times I've wished that I could simply be insensitive. But then my pride kicks in. I want to utilize my strength to take on all the truth I can.

Director: If you are strong enough to know the truth, then you are strong enough to bring yourself in line?

Youth: I don't know if it always works that way. Suppose it did. What pride would come from lining up with truth if it's a given that you can?

Director: You have to try to build your strength in order that you might live up to truth?

Youth: You do.

Director: The given thing is sensitivity, not strength?

Youth: That's right.

Father: But can't a person grow more sensitive?

Youth: You mean to certain things, becoming more aware? I guess. But basically you're sensitive or not.

Director: The sensitivity you're speaking of, is this a thing deriving from the body or the mind?

Youth: It's based in mind.

Director: With body, extra sensitivity can be a sign of sickness, right?

Youth: That's true. But it can also help.

Director: How so?

Youth: If you were sensing something with your skin.

Director: What sort of thing would you so sense?

Youth: There must be something, right? But what about the mind? Do you believe it's illness there that makes for sensitivity?

Director: How could I, friend? We've said that sensitivity involves the truth. Or do you think that other things affect it, too?

Youth: Well, you could be too sensitive to what another says.

Director: You'd need to thicken up your skin?

Youth: You would.

Director: So certain sensitivity might be no good. But sensitivity to truth is good?

Youth: Agreed.

Director: Now let me ask you this. If you are strong and brave and line up with the truth, must good things come your way?

Youth: What's this? Another law?

Father: I like this law. Don't you?

Youth: I think it's more an article of faith. How many times does siding with the truth bring harm? The fight today, where I got hit and fell, how do you think it came about?

Father: If I know you, it was because you stood up for the truth.

Youth: That's right. And it was such a simple, little, stupid truth.

Father: That often is the kind of truth that needs defense. But look what came of it. Our conversation here today. That's good, now, isn't it?

Youth: It is.

Father: And who can say what other good will come? Some of the students who were witness to your stand, some good might come from them. They might admire you. You just don't know.

Youth: And that's exactly why I say it is an article of faith and not a law.

Father: What's wrong with articles of faith? I like all three of ours. If you are strong enough to know, then you are strong enough to do. Your knowledge always makes it possible to act judiciously. If you are strong and brave enough to line up with the truth, good things must come your way. These three are good.

Director: And since they are not given things, we take our chances when we act on them?

Father: That's right. So much of life is taking risks.

Director: What risk is there in thinking you are strong enough to do?

Father: It's possible you're not.

Director: What risk is there in thinking that you'll act judiciously?

Father: It's possible you won't.

Director: What risk is there to think that good might come your way?

Father: You might get something bad instead.

Director: Now, if in all these things you don't get what you want, what then?

Father: You try to learn from how things went and try again.

Youth: You just keep on believing, right?

Father: What's wrong with that? You must have faith.

Youth: But people can be lazy in their faith while thinking that they're being strong.

Director: How are they lazy, Youth?

Youth: They do not try to know the truth. They just believe.

Director: It's hard to know the truth?

Youth: Of course.

Father: But doesn't faith take strength? Why, when you stood up for the truth today that was an act of faith.

Youth: I didn't think that something good would come of it.

Father: Then why did you stand up?

Youth: Because I saw it fell to me.

Father: It fell to you? You mean it was some sort of stroke of destiny?

Youth: I'm not so sure that it was destiny or fate.

Father: You had no reason for your act?

Youth: I simply saw that it was mine to do. Imagine if somebody asked you why you raised your son. You'd simply say that he was yours.

Father: Not simply, no. I'd say I did it out of love.

Youth: Well, I could say the same.

Father: You love to do what falls to you?

Youth: I love to do what's mine and only mine — what's truly mine.

Father: How do you know it's truly yours?

Youth: I feel it in my gut. How's that?

Father: But gut is everything you know and all that you believe. So you believe and know it's yours?

Youth: I do.

Director: You feel as one in knowledge and belief?

Youth: That's right, Director. Yes.

Director: Does this take strength?

Youth: I think it does.

Director: Does all of this just happen in your soul, or is it in your body, too?

Youth: I think that it's in all of me.

Director: How do you know in body, Youth?

Youth: Things just feel right.

Director: How do you know in mind?

Youth: You know through reasoned arguments and through experiments.

Director: But can't we have experiments and arguments for body, too? Or does the body simply know in different ways, in feeling right?

Youth: Experiments and arguments concerning body simply show when you feel right or not.

Director: But can you learn from them?

Youth: Of course.

Director: Does it take strength to learn from them?

Youth: I think it does. You have to brave new things, environments, and see just how you feel.

Director: And when you brave new things you sometimes feel your mind and body aren't in harmony?

Youth: That's true.

Director: Could mind have raced ahead of body and the body must catch up?

Youth: That's possible.

Director: Does it take strength to catch the body up to mind?

Youth: It does.

Director: And what about the other way? Suppose that body is ahead of mind.

Youth: You mean the mind is holding body back?

Director: Suppose the body is quite comfortable in certain situations, but the mind is not.

Youth: Can you give an example here?

Director: Suppose you're at a dance. Your body feels the beat and wants to move. But mentally you're lacking confidence.

Youth: I see. And incidentally, I think we've found the case where it is good for body to be sensitive. It's good to feel the music in your body, right?

Director: Just as it's bad to be unmusical?

Youth: Well, it is bad, but it's not terrible.

Father: I bet it seems quite terrible to those who are.

Youth: I take your point. So where are we? We know that it takes strength to make your mind and body one because at times the mind is far ahead while other times it lags behind, just as the body sometimes leads and lags.

Director: And when we've made the mind and body one, we're strong?

Youth: That's right. And then we feel it in our gut when something must be done because it's ours to do.

Director: You know, I wonder now. Have we discovered one more law, another article of faith, our fourth, that seems much like our first?

Youth: You mean that if we know a thing is ours, we have the strength to do it?

Director: Yes. You stood up for the truth today. You had the strength for that.

Youth: But I got beaten down.

Father: So what? You stood up for the truth, my boy. And that's what counts.

Director: Do you believe you always have the strength for something that belongs to you?

Youth: You mean when I can feel it in my gut, can feel it in my bones? I guess I do. But I believe you cannot know what acting on your gut, your bones, will bring.

Father: How boring if you could!

Director: Do you remember, Youth, the things we said of character and fists?

Youth: I do. We said that strength with fists would make it easier to hold on tight to what you think is right, the building blocks of character.

Director: I wonder now if we were wrong. I mean, today you stood for truth but lost the battle of the fists. And yet your strength of character remains — is even strengthened, no? You didn't need your fists for that.

Youth: That's true. But will I make another stand, aware of what might happen if I do?

Director: Are you suggesting that your body won't align with mind because it is afraid of getting beaten down again?

Youth: Suppose that's true. I wouldn't be as one, and therefore wouldn't feel what's mine to do. I wouldn't recognize when it is time to act. What's worse, what if I move my mind to where my body is? I'd be aligned, alright, but I would be aligned to cowardice, in body and in mind.

Father: Perhaps you only move your body to your mind, and not the other way around.

Youth: But then I might not ever dance, despite the fact I feel the beat.

Director: Your point's well taken, Youth. And this reminds me of a thing we said when we were speaking of the martial arts — the body must obey the mind. Do you believe that's strictly true?

Youth: Not if you ever hope to dance, it's not. The two should be as one.

Director: Your mind can hold you back from something that is fine to do. Your mind can also hold you back from something bad, like cowardice. So what conclusion shall we draw?

Youth: The mind must know what's fine and what is not.

Director: And what about the body, Youth? It, too, must know what's fine?

Youth: Of course.

Director: And did your body know that it was fine to take a punch for truth?

Youth: I guess it did.

Director: And how about your mind?

Youth: It also knew.

Director: Your mind and body were as one, and therefore strong?

Youth: Well, not so strong. I wound up on the ground, you know.

Father: But you were strong enough to make the stand.

Youth: That's true. And with my mind and body one, I'll study martial arts so I can make another, more successful stand.

Director: Do you recall when we first mentioned confidence?

Youth: I do — when we were speaking of the second law, that knowledge makes it possible to act judiciously. You must have confidence to act that way.

Director: What will you do with your new confidence from martial arts?

Youth: I'll act judiciously.

Director: What will that mean?

Youth: That I will do what's mine to do. And I will use restraint. Or else I run the risk of being like the bullies, right?

Director: Are bullies confident?

Youth: They're really not. They're insecure in fundamental ways. They try to act as though they're confident, but go too far.

Director: Restraint takes strength?

Youth: It does. And they lack strength, though they can throw a wicked punch.

Director: So there's no doubt? You'll learn to fight?

Youth: Of course I will.

Director: You want to learn, or you're just doing it?

Youth: I really want to learn.

Director: Will you defend yourself or fight offensively?

Youth: I'll just defend myself.

Director: Do you remember what we said about the man who needs a nudge toward some generosity?

Youth: I do. We said we'd give the nudge.

Director: What if a bully needs a nudge toward more self-restraint?

Youth: I guess I'll give the nudge.

Director: Because you'll have the strength and confidence you'll need?

Youth: That's right.

Father: I think that's fine, as long as it's a nudge and not a shove.

Youth: Don't worry, Dad. I'll use my self-restraint.

Father: You know that things can escalate quite quickly, Youth. You have to be prepared.

Youth: I'll only use a nudge. I don't want trouble any more than you.

Director: Now, Father, I'm impressed. I know how much you love your son, but here you are condoning his offensive thrusts, his taking risks.

Father: You mean that you're surprised I'm not inclined to shelter him? He has to learn to live. A bit of offense is a part of life. But I don't think he'll take that many risks. He'll only act when he is sure the act belongs to him. I trust his gut.

Director: That's good. But what if it takes more than just a nudge to move a bully to restraint?

Father: You mean it takes a fight? Well, fights are part of life. But are you asking me if Youth should start the fight?

Director: Well, there's advantage if the fight is on your terms. Or would you rather that the bully have the upper hand?

Father: In truth? I'd rather Youth would take the fight to him — and win.

Director: Agreed. But are we not forgetting something here? They say a bully always starts the fight.

Youth: That's true. He started it today.

Director: So you can finish it, when you are ready, right?

Youth: That's right. A bully always starts the fight. But I will finish it.

Father: That's good. But let's suppose a bully starts a fight with someone who's a friend. Do you step in and fight?

Youth: I think I'd have to fight.

Father: And let's suppose a bully starts a fight with someone that you barely know. Do you step in and fight?

Youth: I think I'd have to listen to my gut.

Father: And you would listen to your gut when bullies start a fight with people you don't even know?

Youth: I think I'd have to, Dad.

Father: And so it's possible you'll always be in fights once you are really strong enough to fight?

Youth: You'd rather that I always look the other way?

5

Father: That isn't what I'm saying, Youth. It might be yours to fight. But you must never go too far. How often do you think you'll fight?

Youth: At school? Just once or twice. That gets the message out that no one ought to mess with me.

Father: But if you are defending all the others, too?

Youth: Then maybe I'd fight more than that. But please don't worry, Dad. There only are so many bullies at the school. If I can face them down, I've won.

Father: For now, until you go on to the next stage of your life, beyond that school.

Youth: But that's the way it is. Each stage will have its battles, right?

Father: That's true. But can you understand my worries, Youth?

Youth: Of course I can. But I'll grow stronger with each battle that I fight. I'll grow in confidence, assuming that I win. But even if I lose, I'll learn, and live to fight another day.

Director: These battles need not be with fists, correct?

Youth: That's true. I might engage in battles with my wits.

Director: Do you believe there's such a thing as strength of wit? Or do we measure wit another way?

Youth: We say one's wit is slow or quick.

Director: Which one of these is good?

Youth: Why, quick, of course.

Director: Could you be quick but wrong in what you think?

Youth: That's possible.

Director: Could you be slow and right?

Youth: You could.

Director: So which is better, then?

Youth: In that case it is better to be slow.

Director: Because it's better to be right?

Youth: That's right.

Director: It's bad to stumble in your reasoning?

Youth: Of course it is.

Director: Is this most likely when you're going slow or fast?

Youth: I'd say it's likely when you're going fast. But this is only when you're starting out. With time and practice you can build up speed.

Director: While keeping steady, keeping strong, your reasoning?

Youth: Exactly so.

Director: So strength of reasoning's the thing. We always want to keep this strong, no matter if we're slow. But if it's possible to speed things up, we can?

Youth: That's right.

Director: When would we ever want to speed things up? To show how strong we are, that we can reason easily on something hard? We're putting on a show?

Youth: That doesn't sound so good.

Director: And who would understand us, anyway? The others who go fast?

Youth: I guess.

Director: If they are quick all on their own, what need have they for us?

Youth: They don't. Unless they need to know that someone else is fast like them.

Director: You mean so they can know they're not alone?

Youth: Well, that's important, don't you think?

Director: No doubt it is. But I would question why this recognition has to come from speed. Strong reasoning's the thing, we've said. Suppose there's something new to reason on. Would you go fast or slow?

Youth: I'd take it slow.

Director: And if you're strong in reasoning you'd work it through?

Youth: I would.

Director: And who would notice that you'd worked it through?

Youth: Why, everyone who's capable of understanding what I'd done.

Director: And they would give you credit for your reasoning?

Youth: They would — or mostly would.

Director: Why only "mostly would?"

Youth: Some might be jealous, right?

Director: Do you believe the jealous ones might try to start a fight with you?

Youth: They might.

Director: Would you have time to reason slowly as to whether you should join a fight with them?

Youth: I might not have the time. That's why I'd have to listen to my gut.

Director: Your gut speaks instantaneously?

Youth: It does.

Director: Well, maybe we should feed the gut with good, slow reasonings whenever there is time, so that it's ready when it must decide.

Youth: I think that would be best. But what is an example of a reason for the gut?

Father: It's better to be beaten down than lose your values, right?

Youth: That's right.

Father: That's something for the gut.

Youth: But that's not really reasoning. That's simply preference, no?

Director: Don't preferences depend on reasoning?

Youth: Some preferences are merely that, no reasoning involved.

Director: You mean, for instance, you like black and I like blue?

Youth: For instance, sure.

Director: Is that of any consequence to fights?

Youth: It's not.

Director: So tell me something that's of consequence to fights, no reasoning involved.

Youth: You have to stand up for your friends.

Director: That's something you believe, another value that you hold?

Youth: It is.

Director: Now if my memory is right, we said belief can come from thought.

Youth: We did.

Director: And thought is reasoning?

Youth: It is.

Director: It stands to reason that it's best to stand up for your friends?

Youth: Of course it does.

Director: Shall we unfold this reasoning to see exactly what it is you ought to feed your gut?

Youth: No, I know well enough.

Director: Now what if you are reasoning to gut, you're spelling things right out in simple terms, and you discover that you have beliefs that do not stand to reason very well?

Youth: It's possible you'll have to change what you believe.

Director: And this belief, is it so many words, or does it go beyond mere words?

Youth: I guess it goes beyond, just like my father said when speaking of the gut.

Director: Yet reasoning is done with words. How do we reach beyond?

Father: Your gut digests the words you feed to it and turns them into something else.

Youth: But what can words become?

Father: The deeper meaning of the words.

Director: The deeper meaning, friend?

Father: You know. The way you feel about the words.

Director: So if I think of "cat," my gut will tell me how I feel?

Father: That's right.

Youth: But what if you feel nothing for a certain word, a word like "the."

Father: It's my belief that feelings, though they may be slight, attach to every single word we use. We know this when we listen carefully to gut.

Director: Then gut is very powerful.

Father: It truly is.

Director: Do we grow strong the more we listen to our gut?

Father: We do.

Director: And why is that?

Father: And why is that? We're one with how we feel.

Director: Is it the being one that makes us strong?

Father: It is. You're one and indivisible. You can't be turned against yourself.

Director: Well, I, for one, will listen to my gut. What happens, though, if gut sends out conflicting signs?

Father: What do you mean?

Director: I mean, suppose I one day think of "dog" then listen to my gut. My gut sounds fine. But then another day I think of "dog." My gut sounds terrible. What then?

Father: This isn't hard to figure out. Your gut is well aware that there are different sorts of dogs. You have to listen to your gut to know which dogs are which, the kind you want to be around or not.

Director: And that's the way it is with gut for everything?

Father: Exactly so.

Director: So if some words are spoken that would indicate a fight might start, we must be sure to listen to our gut to know the way we feel about the words, and therefore what to do?

Father: That's true.

Director: But let's suppose a bully doesn't use a single word to start a fight. What will our gut say then?

Father: He doesn't have to say a word. The mind has words for what it sees. And so your gut can recognize a bully right away.

Director: From previous experience?

Father: Indeed.

Director: But what if there is something new, a thing or word the mind or gut has never seen or heard before?

Father: Then mind and gut rely on analogues.

Youth: But how can there be analogues to something that's unknown?

Father: You have to go with how it seems.

Youth: But don't appearances at times deceive?

Father: They do. There's nothing to be done.

Director: Might it be better if the gut is silent here, and only speaks when it is sure?

Youth: I think it should be silent. I can't think of anything that's more misleading than a gut that's ill informed.

Director: So let's suppose we find ourselves with silence of the gut. What do we do?

Father: We force ourselves to wait for it to speak. No doubt eventually it will.

Youth: I think we have to take a chance and act, and hope that makes it speak.

Director: Which course would take more strength?

Youth: It takes more strength to act.

Father: It takes more strength to wait.

Director: In either case, for each of you, does it take more because you go against your grain?

Father: Why, yes. It would be easier for me to act.

Youth: It does. I'd rather wait.

Director: What's wrong with doing as you are inclined?

Youth: You take the easy way.

Director: The easy way is always wrong?

Youth: More often times than not.

Director: If gut is silent, Youth, what tells you how you are inclined?

Youth: Why simple habit, I suppose.

Director: And where does habit sit? Is it in heart or mind?

Youth: I'd say that it's in all of you.

Director: It's in your soul and body, both?

Youth: It is.

Director: So when the gut is silent, we just listen to the rest of us?

Youth: Agreed.

Director: Shall we discuss the habits of the body or the habits of the soul?

Youth: Let's talk about the soul.

Director: Can we agree, for argument, that soul is water-like?

Youth: We can.

Director: Can we say habit is a frozen spot, a patch of ice within the soul?

Youth: Of course we can.

Director: To go against the habit is to warm and melt the ice?

Youth: I like this metaphor.

Director: But if we stop our efforts things will cool right down again?

Youth: Agreed. We want our water warm, and that takes effort and great strength. But there's a problem with the metaphor.

Director: I'm sure there is.

Youth: It can't account for habits that are good.

Director: Good habits are at first a matter of some difficulty, yes?

Youth: They are.

Director: They're not the easy way?

Youth: They're not.

Director: But once we've mastered them, are they the easy way? Or would it still be easier to not perform the act that's good?

Youth: It would be easier to not perform the act.

Director: And if we don't perform the act, bad habit ice will creep back in?

Youth: It will. We need to keep things warm by doing good. And that's not easy, I agree.

Father: What kind of habit do we have in mind?

Youth: I know you shave each day. Your habit is to shave. But you have told me that you hate to shave. And yet you do it anyway. You're keeping back the ice.

Father: And that's the good I do? But others like to wear a beard. What ice is there for them?

Youth: I'm sure they have their ice. We all have ice we have to fight.

Director: There only are three certainties — our taxes, death, and ice?

Youth: That's right. And ice is creeping death.

Director: But are we saying here that we're inclined to let the ice creep in? That this is easier?

Youth: It certainly is easier.

Director: Yet we three are inclined, ironically enough, to go against that inclination, yes?

Youth: We are.

Director: But all of this is only when the gut is silent, right? I mean, if gut could speak would it not speak against the ice? Or do I have it wrong?

Youth: No, I believe you have it right. But I would say it's hard at times to act on what you hear from gut.

Director: Is that when gut has got no ally in the soul?

Youth: What sort of ally would it have?

Director: The character.

Youth: You mean when gut and character agree you'll almost certainly perform the act in question, right?

Director: That's right, if you are listening to gut.

Father: And harmony of character and gut is most important when the act in question is quite difficult. Don't you agree?

Youth: Of course I do.

Director: The gut supports the character and character supports the gut?

Youth: That's how it ought to be.

Director: If one is strong and one is weak, what happens then?

Youth: You might not do what you should do.

Director: What happens to your character if you don't do what you should do?

Youth: It weakens, right?

Director: A weakened character is not inclined to take on things that are quite difficult?

Youth: That's true.

Director: Now tell me this. Do you see any problem with a character that's very, very strong?

Youth: Not in the character itself, I don't.

Director: What problem do you see?

Youth: A character like that can be a lightning rod.

Director: The lightning comes from those who're weak in character?

Youth: It does.

Director: But are we saying that the weak attack the strong?

Youth: Not all the weak, but yes.

Director: But do they do this on their own?

Youth: They don't. They gang up on the strong.

Director: What makes them hate the strong of character, if hate is not too strong a word?

Youth: No, hate is what it is. I think it's all because of jealousy.

Director: And that's what makes a man a lightning rod?

Youth: What really brings the lightning on is when he's openly superior to weaker men.

Director: I see. What stops the weak from being strong themselves?

Youth: They don't have values that they hold with all their might.

Director: They let their values go?

Youth: They do.

Director: For what?

Youth: For ease, I guess. When things get tough they just let go. And so they hate the ones that hold on tight through thick and thin.

Director: But why? It's clear that they prefer their ease. Why can't they just accept that someone else does not?

Youth: I think it's all because the strong of character succeed in life, and they do not.

Director: What makes the strong succeed?

Youth: They are dependable. You know what you will get with them.

Director: What else?

Youth: They're honest and hardworking, too.

Director: You're speaking of a character that's good. Can evil characters be lightning rods, as well?

Youth: No, I don't think they can. An evil character is always weak.

Director: The character itself, perhaps. But what about the man? Suppose he is quite treacherous. Suppose he lies, and cheats, and steals with skill. Suppose, in sum, that he's as evil as can be. Do you believe this man is always weaker than the man who has good character? In other words, is character alone enough to win the fight?

Youth: It's nice to think a man of character will always win. But I'm not sure that's how it goes.

6

Director: What can be done? Is there a way to weaken evil men?

Youth: I think you have to catch them up, expose them for exactly what they are. That weakens them.

Director: Do you expose them only to yourself?

Youth: Of course you don't. You must expose them to as many people as you can.

Director: Just anyone?

Youth: The people we expose the evil to are good.

Director: And do the good do something to the evil men who're so exposed?

Youth: They shun them, at the least.

Director: And does this matter to an evil man?

Youth: Well, maybe not. But people who are good can do much more than that.

Director: Because the good, combined, are always stronger than an evil one?

Youth: I think that in the aggregate they're always stronger than the strongest evil one.

Director: And why is that?

Youth: It's simply something I believe.

Father: I think we've found another law, or article of faith — our fifth.

Director: The trick is banding all the good as one?

Youth: It is.

Director: But what about the evil, Youth? Can't they band up as well? And who is stronger then?

Youth: The problem for the evil is they don't much like to band.

Director: The people who are good, are they inclined to band?

Youth: More so than evil people, yes.

Director: What does it take for them to band against a foe?

Youth: They have to see the danger that they're in.

Director: And that's enough?

Youth: I think it is.

Director: But they don't always see?

Youth: It's funny you should ask. At school, if all the good would join, they'd put the bullies down.

Director: And yet they don't. Why not?

Youth: I guess that most of them just live in hope the bullies will not turn on them.

Director: They think it's not their problem, right — until it is?

Youth: It's sad but true.

Director: Now there is something puzzling here. The good don't seem inclined to band until they're forced. And yet the bullies in your school have banded naturally. Perhaps the evil like to band.

Youth: Well, maybe I was wrong.

Director: There might be something more to what you said. Does banded good prevail against a banded evil foe?

Youth: You mean must good prevail, as if by some necessity?

Director: What do you think?

Youth: Director, I'm not sure that's always so, no matter what I'd like to think.

Director: What makes one side prevail?

Youth: The side that has the greater force will win, regardless if it's evil or it's good.

Director: Suppose the greater force makes grave mistakes. What then?

Youth: It cannot be the greater force. It's part of being strong to make no grave mistakes.

Director: We've come around to strength of mind, to judgment, in this case?

Youth: We have.

Director: Now let's review what we are saying here. The greater force will always win. But force is more than muscle mass. It's in the mind as well.

Youth: Just so.

Director: But force is also in the bonds between the men arrayed, correct?

Youth: Correct.

Director: Where would you say those bonds exist?

Youth: For them to be as strong as possible? They have to be within the heart.

Director: Now, what about the evil ones? When they are bonded to each other are the bonds within their hearts?

Youth: I'm certain that they're not.

Director: How are the evil bonded then?

Youth: I guess they're bonded merely with their minds.

Director: The simple reasoning is that I'm stronger with these others so I'll stand with them?

Youth: I think that's it.

Director: Now what about the good who're bonded by the heart?

Youth: Their bond is love.

Director: The good must love each other then?

Youth: That's right. They love the others' qualities of character because they have the same.

Father: It's love of self extended to the love of those who're like.

Director: But, Father, can't the evil ones love those who're just like them?

Father: But they don't love themselves. In fact, I sometimes think they hate themselves.

Director: So love's the difference?

Father: Yes. The good will conquer through the power of love.

Director: Now, what's the biggest fight there is?

Father: Well, that would be a war.

Director: Is love enough to win a war?

Father: You know, it just might be. It's love that keeps the fighting spirit up. And that's the goal of war — to break the spirit of the enemy, his will to fight. Of course, it helps to have good weapons and supplies. And training never hurts.

Director: The good will fight by means of love, and evil men will fight by what?

Father: By means of hate.

Director: Suppose that leadership and weapons and supplies and training are in equal part distributed to evil and to good. And let's suppose the numbers of each side are equal, too. Who wins? The evil or the good?

Father: The good, by virtue of their love.

Director: But if the evil are numerically superior?

Father: Then they might win.

Director: And so on with their weapons and supplies? If they are far superior they may well win?

Father: That's right.

Director: But all things being equal, love will always win.

Father: In every case. And even if the good men lose the war, their love can make it possible for them to win the peace.

Director: So why is love more powerful than hate? Is it because the heart is stronger than the mind?

Father: Not quite. It is because the heart and mind combined are stronger than the mind alone.

Director: The evil only use their minds? Is that because their hearts are bad?

Father: Their hearts are rotten, yes.

Director: What makes a rotten heart?

Father: The heart's a muscle, right? Well, you must exercise your heart by holding on, by being true. The evil men aren't true.

Director: But can't an evil man hold on to hate deep down within his heart?

Father: He can. But hate is cancerous. It eats the heart. And so the evil man is only left with mind.

Director: And mind without support from heart is bad?

Father: It has to be. It's all adrift.

Director: What happens to a man with rotten heart and drifting mind?

Father: He cannot form attachments properly.

Director: You mean like bonds of love.

Father: I do.

Director: But what about the force of will? Can't this serve as an anchor to an evil man?

Father: I think you're on to something there.

Director: We said a thing or two about the will. Do you remember what?

Father: We said that will is holding on to what you want.

Youth: And thinking, too. We said you have to think. That's how you know the things to want.

Director: But now I'm wondering. Can't you just feel the things you want, no thought involved?

Father: Of course you can.

Director: So this is how it goes? We feel a thing we want. We think about the way to get this thing. And then we set our will to follow down the course that leads us to the thing.

Father: That's certainly the way it goes.

Youth: So you don't think it's possible to want a thing based on your thoughts alone?

Director: Well, thoughts can lead to feelings, right?

Youth: They can.

Director: So then we think, then feel, then think again, and then we set our will?

Youth: I think that's how it goes.

Director: Alright. Now what about the anchor of the evil man? Do we still think it's will?

Father: We do.

Youth: But what's the anchor of a good man, Dad?

Father: A good man's anchor is his heart.

Youth: Then what's his will?

Father: It's his determination to support his heart.

Director: What happens if a person's will does not support his heart?

Father: His life is difficult. The heart holds on, but gets no help.

Director: And that is even though the mind, distinguished from the will, supports the heart?

Father: If thinking by itself could make things so, the world would be a different place. You must have will to back your thoughts.

Youth: I understand. But I have got a problem with our metaphor. Suppose we don't just want to sit at anchor, Dad. Suppose we want to sail. What then?

Father: Your heart becomes your compass, Youth.

Youth: And what's your mind?

Father: Your chart.

Youth: And what's your will?

Father: The effort that it takes to stay on course. How's that?

Youth: That's not too bad. So when an evil man sets sail he lacks a working compass, then? How does he steer?

Father: He keeps within clear sight of land.

Youth: So he can't cross the sea?

Father: Let's say he can't — at least not on his own.

Youth: You mean that he might follow someone good?

Father: That happens, yes.

Youth: The rotten hearted cannot make their way alone across the sea. If they weren't evil I would think that's sad.

Father: What's sad is when they knock a good man off his course.

Youth: But why would they do that? Don't they intend to cross the sea with him?

Father: It happens when they've all but crossed and see the other shore. In sight of land the evil man is in his element again.

Youth: Then why not simply go and leave the better man alone?

Father: He hates the better man for being better, Youth. The evil man would wreck the good man's ship.

Youth: And how does he do this?

Father: He offers him false reasonings.

Youth: You mean he offers him a chart that is inaccurate?

Father: That's right. He must persuade the better man that what he's using for a chart is wrong.

Youth: And all of this in sight of shore? The good man sees the coast. How hard is it to steer toward port? Why does he need the chart?

Father: You can't forget there might be hidden rocks or reefs, my boy.

Youth: And so the good man doubts his chart, makes use of what the evil man declares is true, and he is lost — his ship is torn apart?

Father: That's right.

Director: What makes the evil strong in preying on our doubts?

Father: They make a study of these doubts. They're fascinated by our goodness and they want to find the flaw. To someone long in evil many of the good are easy marks. We have to watch ourselves.

Youth: What leverage do they have?

Father: The good are usually embarrassed by their flaws, involuntary flaws. The evil can exploit this shame.

Youth: So how do you defend yourself against the evil ones?

Father: You must accept that you have flaws. It's just a fact of life. You cannot let a shame for them be turned on you.

Youth: The best defense is having nothing to defend, no shame?

Father: That's true. But if you have got shame, you have to let it go.

Youth: That's it? Just let it go? What if it's really bad?

Father: You learn from it, then act on what you've learned — then let it go.

Youth: I fear that I'm an easy mark. I know that I have flaws, and I admit that I'm ashamed of them. I'm pretty good at holding on, but when it comes to letting go, I'm not.

Director: What sort of strength does letting go require?

Youth: I guess that it takes confidence.

Director: Do you remember what we said it takes to build your confidence?

Youth: We said that it takes time. You have to train it gradually. You take a step, and then another step, and then another step.

Father: But don't forget you have to stop and rest.

Youth: That's right. You have to stop and rest. And then you step some more, increasing what you do.

Director: Do you believe you have to build your confidence?

Youth: I do.

Director: Are you prepared to take a step?

Youth: I am.

Director: What sort of step?

Youth: For one, I'm going to study martial arts.

Director: And this will give you confidence?

Youth: It will. And so will standing up to any bully at my school.

Director: And what will happen if they start a fight with you?

Youth: I'll fight.

Director: And if you lose?

Youth: I guess I'll have to lick my wounds and train to fight again.

Director: And if you lose again?

Youth: I'll do the same. I won't give up.

Director: And that will build your confidence?

Youth: I think it will.

Director: Despite the fact you lose?

Youth: The only shame is failing to put up a fight.

Director: Can you remember that, if someone tries to take advantage of whatever shame you feel?

Youth: I'll try. I'll have to fight whoever would manipulate my flaws.

Father: And that's a battle that you can't afford to lose, the only one where fighting's not enough. You simply have to win.

Youth: And everything depends on confidence, the confidence of letting go? What happens if I lose my nerve and fail, and someone evil gets a hold of me?

Father: Your soul's in hock, until you find the strength to free yourself by letting go your shame.

Youth: But all of this assumes I'm good, that all my shame is innocent.

Father: That's right, it does.

Youth: And what about the evil ones? Don't they have flaws?

Director: Of course they do. But let me share with you a thing I've heard. The evil ones, instead of, or along with, feeling shame for any flaw that they might have, feel jealousy and hate. What do you think of that?

Father: I think it's true.

Director: Do you believe it's possible to choose what you will feel?

Youth: I don't. I had no choice in how I felt when I was on the ground today. I was ashamed, and that was all I was.

Father: I thought that you felt proud for standing up for truth.

Youth: I did, until I fell. The point, however, is that jealousy and hate were furthest from my mind.

7

Director: Is jealousy a thing that good can feel for evil, Youth?

Youth: No, I don't think it is.

Director: So you're not jealous of the bullies at your school?

Youth: Of course I'm not.

Director: And what of hate?

Youth: You're asking if I hate the ones who bully me? The truth is that I don't, though I suppose I have good reason to.

Director: But if you have good reason it would seem you ought to hate. Or maybe you don't have good reason, Youth.

Father: Well, even if there's reason for it, I'd discourage hate.

Director: Can you say why?

Father: I think that hate distracts you from the task at hand.

Director: And what is needed for the task at hand?

Father: A cold, clear mind — a mind prepared to fight.

Director: So are we saying then that good should not hate evil?

Youth: Maybe we should say the good can't let their hate for evil get the upper hand.

Director: So it's alright to hate, as long as it does not become a raging fire, threatening your mind? Now evil men, do they feel hate?

Youth: Of course they do.

Director: Do they allow the hate to get the upper hand?

Youth: I think they do.

Director: But can't the evil be quite cold and calculating?

Youth: Yes, I think that's true.

Director: And that is through their strength of mind?

Youth: I guess.

Director: So now they seem just like the good? They hate, but bear their hate so that it isn't threatening the mind?

Youth: There has to be a difference here.

Director: Do you believe it's in the quality of hate?

Youth: No, hate is hate no matter who the hater is.

Director: Well then, perhaps it's in the reason for the hate.

Youth: That's it! The difference is that evil men start out with hate for those who're good, from jealousy. They act on it.

Director: They harm the good?

Youth: They do. And when the good are harmed, they start to hate in turn.

Director: Are you one of the good?

Youth: I like to think I am.

Director: You've had some evil ones work harm on you?

Youth: I have.

Director: And yet you do not hate?

Youth: Well, maybe it takes time to grow — at least for me.

Director: And maybe if and when it's grown you'll take revenge? Or do you think it's possible to have revenge without a trace of hate?

Youth: I'm not so sure.

Director: Do you believe revenge is justice, Youth?

Youth: I think it can be, yes.

Director: Is justice cold?

Youth: I think it is.

Director: But hatred can be cold, as well?

Youth: It can.

Director: Now, as we've noted, evil men are sometimes cold.

Youth: But they do not have justice on their side.

Director: So justice differentiates the evil from the good?

Youth: It does. And that's because the evil work their harm completely unprovoked.

Director: Did you provoke the one who fought with you today?

Youth: Well, that's the thing. I sort of did. I stood up for the truth. He was provoked by that.

Director: You knew you would provoke the boy by doing that?

Youth: I had a good idea I would.

Director: But good ideas don't make for knowledge, Youth.

Youth: You're right. I didn't know.

Director: The goddess Justice, would she say that you were in the wrong for standing by the truth, provoking as you did?

Youth: She wouldn't, no.

Director: You'd say that she was on your side?

Youth: I would.

Director: Do you believe that she is with you now?

Youth: As much as I believe in goddesses, I do.

Director: Do you believe in justice, Youth?

Youth: At times it seems injustice rules the world.

Director: Now, do you hate injustice, or are you just neutral when it comes to this?

Youth: I hate injustice, yes.

Director: You hate injustice everywhere?

Youth: I do.

Director: And evil men hate justice everywhere?

Youth: They do — especially when it is done to them.

Director: What makes them hate the just?

Youth: Aside from jealousy? They think they're hypocrites.

Director: Can you say more?

Youth: They think the just is simply the advantage of the strong.

Director: You mean the good, the just, make rules of conduct favoring themselves, when they are strong, then say they must apply across the board, to everyone?

Youth: Exactly so. The evil ones don't think it's fair.

Father: Of course it's fair. Our laws and moral codes apply with equal force to all. The truth is that the evil want the laws and codes to favor them!

Director: And that would be unjust?

Father: Indeed.

Director: Now, Youth, you said you hate injustice, yes?

Youth: I did.

Director: Do you hate evil, too? Or are you really neutral there?

Youth: No, I'm not neutral there.

Director: You hate all evil everywhere?

Youth: I do.

Director: Do you believe that evil and injustice are the same?

Youth: Well, if they're not, there is a lot of overlap.

Director: Do you believe it's better if you hate the evil and unjust in theory or in fact?

Youth: I don't know what you mean.

Director: I mean, do you believe the boy who punched you in the nose today was either evil or unjust to you?

Youth: I do.

Director: So do you hate this boy, this fact?

Youth: I . . . don't.

Director: Then you hate evil and injustice everywhere, except when it applies to you?

Youth: No, that's not true.

Director: Well, maybe you don't really think that boy is either evil or unjust.

Youth: But I believe he is.

Director: Then you don't really hate the evil or unjust?

Youth: But how can I say that?

Director: You can, because it seems you have no need for hate.

Father: Do people ever really have a need for hate?

Youth: The evil do.

Director: What do they need it for?

Youth: To overcome their shame.

Director: And what about the good? How do they overcome their shame? Do they use hate?

Youth: No, they use love.

Director: Their love will give them confidence enough to let go shame?

Youth: I like to think it will.

Director: So tell me how their confidence derives from love.

Youth: Well, it can come from who and what they love — their family and friends; themselves and those like them, whoever they might be; and finally the truth.

Director: So loving is enough to make you let go shame?

Father: Not loving by itself. You must be loved in turn.

Director: The truth can love you back?

Father: No, not the truth. The people that you love.

Director: And so reciprocated love will give you confidence? Or should I say that it encourages that step of confidence you have to take all on your own?

Father: That's more the thing.

Director: Then it would seem that Youth has failed to take his step. And why do I say that? He felt ashamed today, despite reciprocated love from you, my friend. Or do I have it wrong?

Youth: Well, maybe I need more encouragement.

Director: You mean that love is not enough? What could it take?

Youth: A victory.

Director: You mean that if you're strong enough to win you won't feel shame?

Youth: Of course.

Director: Your weakness is the flaw that you must overcome?

Youth: That's right.

Director: And when you do what will you feel?

Youth: I will feel pride.

Director: And pride and shame are incompatible?

Youth: Without a doubt.

Director: Do you believe it's possible to fight with pride?

Youth: I do.

Director: What does it take to fight with pride?

Youth: You have to fight a proper fight.

Director: A proper fight? What's that?

Youth: It's one where you do nothing shameful, right?

Director: I see. What happens if you fight a proper fight and lose? Or will you tell me that it's always shameful if you lose?

Youth: It's better if you win.

Director: It's better if you win by shameful means?

Youth: Of course it isn't, no.

Director: So winning can't be all that counts?

Youth: That's true.

Director: It's clear it matters how you fight. Does it much matter why you fight?

Youth: It matters very much.

Director: So when a good man fights, what is the reason why he fights?

Youth: He fights because of what he loves.

8

Director: And what about the evil, Youth?

Youth: They fight because of what they hate.

Director: And just so we're completely clear — the good will always fight from love?

Youth: They will, as long as they are good.

Director: Now if you fight from love, do you believe that love will always give you greater strength? Or does an evil man have greater strength when fighting from his hate? Let's set aside the notion of the banding of the evil or the good. What happens with the individual, alone?

Youth: We said that when the good combine their hearts and minds they're stronger than the evil who just use their minds alone. But I believe the evil use their hearts, their hateful hearts, as well. And yet I somehow feel that love will give the greater strength, a strength that can sustain you, even when you're fighting on your own.

Father: Perhaps this is another article of faith, our sixth?

Director: I'd like to modify that article a bit, my friend. Let's say that love will give you greater strength, but it requires greater strength as well.

Youth: What makes you say it takes more strength to fight from love than hate?

Director: Does it not seem much harder to defend a precious thing than merely to attack? The good defend the objects of their love. They're always on the watch. The evil men are unattached, attacking where and when they will. Is it not easier to fight that way?

Youth: It is. But we must take the fight to them, not simply wait for their attack.

Director: But always with an eye to justice, Youth?

Youth: Of course. The good will always fight with justice on their side.

Director: And does this make them stronger, too?

Youth: I think it does. But this is part of why it's harder for the good to fight.

Director: You mean that it takes strength in order to be just?

Youth: I do. The just must exercise restraint — and that takes strength.

Director: The evil men are free from this?

Youth: They are — and that is an advantage and a disadvantage both.

Director: Because there is a strength that comes from justice, yes?

Youth: There is.

Director: Both love and justice take our strength but give us strength in turn?

Youth: They amplify the strength they take and give it back in force.

Director: And so the good, as long as they are fighting both with justice and with love, are always stronger than the evil ones?

Father: All other factors being equal, yes.

Director: It seems it's settled, then. The good, when they are being good, are strong. What makes the evil strong?

Youth: Essentially? The force of all their hate, and nothing else.

Director: What would it take to make the evil weak?

Youth: Can we dilute their hate?

Father: And how might we do that? Should we be nice to them?

Youth: Of course we shouldn't, no. It wouldn't matter if we were. They'd hate us all the more.

Director: So is there nothing we can do?

Youth: I can't see what.

Director: Then it appears that we must fight them in their strength. But tell me, now. Can evil men dilute a good man's justice or his love?

Youth: Well, I can see how they might tempt him to become unjust. It's hard to fight an enemy with one hand tied behind your back. You want to use them both, both right and left. But love? The only way the evil men can touch him there is if they get him drunk on hate. His love must always rule his heart or he has lost the fight, has lost what he is fighting for.

Director: The same is true of justice then? If he becomes unjust he's lost the fight, has lost what he is fighting for?

Youth: That's right. A good man fights for justice and for love.

Director: This dual source of strength, is it as one? In other words, do love and justice always go together, Youth?

Youth: I think they do.

Director: And why is that?

Youth: You love a friend because he's good, and part of being good is being just. You also love yourself for being just.

Director: A good man can't imagine loving someone who's unjust?

Youth: He can't.

Director: Do you believe the evil love a man they know to be unjust?

Youth: The evil don't love anyone — at least not in the way that I mean love. But they most certainly would use a man like that, a man who is unjust.

Director: They'd use him for their loveless, evil ends?

Youth: Exactly so.

Director: What are the evil's ends?

Youth: They want to wreck the good, by any means.

Director: And take their place?

Youth: I think they do. They're jealous, after all. But they are in for one surprise! They haven't got a clue what love and justice mean, the things it truly takes to take the place of good.

Director: So this would be a comedy, if it were not so very sad?

Youth: I think you're right. The evil ones would fumble helplessly in their attempt to rule.

Director: To rule? Is that what this is all about?

Father: Essentially, it is.

Director: Both good and evil wish to rule?

Father: Of course they do. That is the ultimate expression of your strength.

Director: A good man rules with justice while a bad man rules without?

Father: Exactly so.

Director: And it takes strength to rule with justice?

Father: Yes.

Director: Strong men must rule for justice to prevail?

Father: Indeed.

Director: And if the weaker rule, they'll likely be unjust?

Father: That's right.

Director: Unjust to all, or only to the good?

Father: Unjust to all.

Director: Unjust to their good friends?

Youth: The evil do not have good friends.

Director: The weaker sort are "evil" now?

Youth: When they're unjust, they are.

Director: Unjust to their associates?

Father: Unjust to their associates.

Director: Then how are they to rule?

Father: They turn whatever entity they rule into a tyranny.

Director: I thought you said these men were weak.

Father: They are.

Director: But doesn't it take strength to run a tyranny?

Youth: I think Director's right. We have to work this through. The tyrants are quite strong. If they were not, they'd never rule.

Director: And how do tyrants rule?

Youth: They have their slaves, of course. But they're unjust to them.

Director: They rule the slaves the way they rule the rest, through jealousy and hate?

Youth: If they are evil men, they do.

Director: You think it's possible that they're not evil men?

Youth: No, they're as evil as they come. And they are really strong.

Director: But can you rule through hate and jealousy alone?

Youth: No, they have something more — their strength of will, the anchor of an evil man.

Director: So tyrants somehow took control and cast their anchors down. Do we have any hope that love and justice will prevail?

Youth: If all the good could band together, yes.

Director: Well, what's to stop them, then?

Youth: In tyranny nobody is allowed to band.

Director: You seem to know a lot concerning tyranny.

Youth: We studied it in school.

Director: So no one is allowed to band. What are the good to do?

Youth: They band in secret and they plot to overthrow the tyrants and their slaves.

Director: Through simple force of love and justice?

Youth: Yes, but that is not enough.

Director: What do they need?

Youth: A way into the tyrants' lair.

Director: They're going to kill the tyrants?

Youth: Yes.

Director: Then they will rule?

Youth: They will restore the old regime.

Director: I see. But what if much has changed so that the old regime is obsolete?

Youth: Then they must form a new regime.

Director: What happens to the slaves? Are they to be redeemed?

Youth: Oh, no. They must be put to death.

Director: To death?

Youth: There is no hope for them. They're evil past repair. They served the tyrants far too long.

Director: But if they only served a little while?

Youth: The tyrants chose these slaves because they're evil men.

Director: You're saying that the good would never serve the tyranny.

Youth: The good would never, ever serve.

Director: Because they're strong in love and justice?

Youth: Yes.

Director: And justice for the tyrants and their men is death.

Youth: That's right.

Director: Well, there's an end to it. Now what about the evil men in normal times? What punishment for them?

Youth: The punishment that's just, of course.

Director: What punishment for those who bully you?

Youth: Once I am trained, when they start fights with me, I'll beat them up.

Director: What punishment for those who pick on friends of yours?

Youth: I'll stand up for my friends, and if the bullies challenge me, we'll fight.

Director: And if you lose?

Youth: Then I will try again.

Director: And if you lose again? What justice is there, Youth?

Youth: Some of the other students who are witness to the fights might be inclined to turn against the ones who beat me up.

Director: The banding of the good.

Youth: That's right. They say what goes around will come around, and I believe it's true.

Director: I thought you said it seems injustice rules the world.

Youth: I said it seems that way at times.

Director: You're feeling strong in justice here?

Youth: I am. We three are strong in justice, yes.

Director: Are you afraid of what will happen when you're all alone?

Youth: I have my friends.

Director: That's good. And they are strong?

Youth: Well, some of them are fairly strong. But some are fairly weak.

Director: Do you believe that you are weak?

Youth: No, I believe that I am pretty strong.

Director: Just pretty strong? You stood up for the truth. That took real strength.

Youth: But then I took a punch and fell. I was ashamed.

Director: But you're ashamed no more?

Youth: That's right — at least not here. I'm not sure how it's going to be at school.

Director: The bullies and some of the other students will make fun of you?

Youth: I think they will.

Director: These other students, are they good?

Youth: How could they be?

Director: But are they evil, then?

Youth: I don't know that I'd call them that. I'm not sure that their hearts are filled with hate.

Director: Then why will they make fun of you?

Youth: Oh, I don't know. I guess they're bored.

Director: And you're the entertainment of the day? Their need for entertainment, what's it all about?

Youth: I think that it's a sign of ignorance.

Director: What sort of ignorance?

Youth: They don't know how to entertain themselves.

Director: Can they be taught?

Youth: I think that it's too late for them.

Director: But they are young.

Youth: Not in their hearts.

Director: The young at heart don't feel such need for entertainment, then, if that is what it is?

Youth: They don't. They're never bored.

Director: What do they do to keep the boredom off?

Youth: They read, for one.

Director: And reading, in and of itself, is good?

Youth: Well, I don't know. An evil man can love to read.

Director: But evil men aren't young at heart?

Youth: Agreed.

Director: The younger hearts, are they much stronger than the older sort?

Youth: They are.

Director: What makes them strong?

Youth: Well, they're just strong. And they are flexible.

Director: Is flexibility a sign of strength?

Youth: Of course it is. When hearts are flexible they're capable of holding on to what they care about through any change that comes their way.

Director: The students who'll make fun of you, they can't hold on to what they care about when there is change?

Youth: They can't.

Director: And younger hearts, when they encounter change, do they, while holding on, both learn and grow?

Youth: Of course.

Director: And what about the older hearts?

Youth: They have no strong desire to learn. They think that they already know.

Director: Already know? Know what?

Youth: The way that life must be. That's why they're old at heart. Life seems predictable to them.

Director: And that is why they crave whatever sort of entertainment they can find?

Youth: I think that's how it is.

Director: So you put on a show for them when you were beaten up. You'd think that they'd be grateful, right?

Youth: I think that they despise my standing up for truth.

Director: Why would they, Youth?

Youth: Because they think they know that it's not possible to stand up for the truth — at least not possible without results like mine.

Director: They think you met with justice?

Youth: Yes. They think I got my just deserts.

Director: I don't much care for how they think of justice, then. But tell me this. Do you believe that truth belongs most properly to those who're young at heart?

Youth: I do. The young hold on to it no matter what.

Director: So they must stand up to the mockery.

Youth: They must.

Director: And if they do, they might unsettle some of those who're old at heart?

Youth: They might.

Director: What happens when the old at heart are shaken up?

Youth: I think that they resent the ones who shook them up.

Director: Resentment is a lot like hate.

Youth: You think the old at heart are always evil, then?

Director: If they are dominated by their hate, it seems that's what we're saying here, at least when they are shaken up.

Father: The young at heart are good. It's easy to agree with this. But are they wise?

Youth: I think they can be wise.

Father: Well, what is wisdom, Youth?

Youth: It's being strong enough to hold on to the things we love, against all odds. The young at heart are best at this.

Director: So wisdom of the heart is strength?

Youth: It is.

Director: And what about the wisdom of the mind?

Youth: I think that it's the same.

Director: Can reading help to make you strong in mind?

Youth: It can.

Director: And is that so for both the good and evil, Youth?

Youth: I guess.

Director: What do the evil like to read? Young hearted tales of love?

Youth: The good would read a book like that.

Director: And would they also read heroic tales of courage towards the truth?

Youth: They would.

Director: Then what do evil men enjoy?

Youth: The sort of thing that amplifies their hate.

Director: I see. So when the young at heart take up a book, it amplifies their love?

Youth: That's right. They look for books like that.

Director: Now, how does anybody know what sort of book they've got until they've read it through?

Youth: Well, you can tell.

Director: How so?

Youth: You hear about the book. You read about the book. You scan a chapter in the store. That's how you know.

Director: Then there is no surprise?

Youth: It's possible to think you'll like a book and then you find you really love the book. It works the other way around, as well. So you can be surprised.

9

Director: Do you believe that there can be a book that both the good and evil love?

Youth: I don't.

Director: Because the evil and the good have different tastes?

Youth: To put it mildly, yes.

Director: Then tell me this. Suppose a person loves a book that's good, a book that's meant to amplify the love within your heart. Do you believe this person necessarily is good? In other words, are books the touchstone of the man?

Youth: Can you tell good or evil from a book? I'd like to think you can. But no, I don't believe it's possible.

Director: Why not?

Youth: The evil can, at times, be sentimental.

Director: What does that entail?

Youth: It makes it seem they love good books. But it's just empty sentiment. It's not real love.

Director: How can you tell real love from empty sentiment?

Youth: The ones who truly love live up to what they love within the books. At least they try. The ones with empty sentiment don't think it's possible to live like that. It's just a fantasy for them.

Director: It's merely entertainment, then?

Youth: That's right. They see no morals to the books, no lessons to be learned.

Director: So never simply judge a man by all the books he's read and claims to love.

Youth: That's good advice.

Director: Does it take strength to live up to the moral of a book?

Youth: Of course it does.

Director: And this is moral strength?

Youth: It is.

Director: But tell me this. Do people learn the way to live from books? Or do the people know the way before they read?

Youth: I'm not sure which comes first. If they don't know, I guess they learn. If they already know, then what they know is reinforced. In either case, the point is that the book feels relevant. You can relate to what's inside.

Director: It resonates?

Youth: That is precisely what it does.

Director: Just what exactly resonates?

Youth: The values that the book contains.

Director: And if you learn or reinforce a value from a book, you'd say you took the book to heart?

Youth: I think that puts it well.

Director: So books have character.

Youth: You're right. They do.

Director: When you choose friends, you choose them by their character?

Youth: I think that's most important, yes.

Director: And that's the way it is with books?

Youth: It is.

Director: You love good character, wherever it is found.

Youth: I do.

Director: And character takes strength?

Youth: That's right. You have to hold your values tight.

Director: So certain books are strong?

Youth: They are.

Director: Are they expressions of the writers' strength?

Youth: A wonderful expression, yes.

Director: Now, Father, you told us that rule's the ultimate expression of your strength. Do you remember that?

Father: Of course I do.

Director: Do you still hold to that?

Father: You're asking me if writing books can be as hard as ruling over men?

Director: What do you think?

Father: A book of character, a solid book, is hard to write.

Director: And what of those who walk the walk, whose characters are solid as a solid book?

Father: It's very hard to have a solid character.

Director: Because it is a sort of rule?

Father: It's rule of self, indeed.

Youth: What sort of rule is there in writing books?

Father: I'd say it's rule of craft, one's art.

Director: Does it take men of solid character to write good books of solid character?

Father: It does.

Director: Can you say why that is?

Father: There must be something that sustains an author as he writes. An evil man would never last through all the effort that a book like that would take. But as a good man writes, the values he sets down will resonate with those he holds and thus inspire him. His very art sustains him as he goes.

Director: And how do men of solid character sustain themselves?

Father: Through family and friends, and books that resonate.

Director: And how do evil men sustain themselves?

Father: Through working harm to men who're good, to men of character.

Youth: But can destructiveness alone sustain? Is there no resonance?

Father: The evil have no love that can sustain, no resonance. To them it's all about the thrill.

Youth: Then why don't they burn out if they are merely living thrill to thrill?

Father: It takes no strength to live like that. If you expend no strength you can't burn out.

Director: How do the good expend their strength?

Father: By holding on to love and values, as we've said.

Director: Does holding on make good men deep in soul?

Father: Precisely so.

Director: So evil men are shallower?

Father: They only skim the surface of this life.

Youth: They skip along like water bugs from thrill to thrill?

Father: That's right.

Director: But don't the good enjoy a thrill from time to time?

Father: They do. But it's a different sort of thrill.

Director: How so?

Father: They rise up from the depths and touch or break the surface, then go down again. It is a playful sort of thrill, a bit of levity.

Youth: How often do they play like this?

Father: Oh, quite a bit — whenever there's no threat from evil men.

Director: But when there is a threat?

Father: They're deadly serious.

Youth: What happens if they're not? What happens if they play when evil men are near?

Father: The evil men can catch them up.

Youth: In nets of evil lies?

Father: Exactly that. They make the good forget.

Youth: Forget the good down in the depths? But how can that be possible?

Father: Some good get dazzled in their play. They feel how easy life upon the surface is.

Youth: But it can't last?

Father: That's right, my son. But they don't know this at the time. And then the evil come, and make their arguments.

Youth: What do they say?

Father: They say that those who live down in the depths are fools. They ought to spend their lives in play, not holding on.

Youth: And that persuades some of the good?

Father: The argument is much embellished by the evil men. But that's its essence, and it is enough to turn some of the good.

Youth: And once they're turned they only care for thrill?

Father: That's right, although at first they think that thrill is play.

Youth: So it's an evil transformation of the innocence of play.

Father: It is. And do you know how this occurs? The muscles used for holding on begin to atrophy while on the surface, Youth. The evil men are well aware of this. They wait. And when they see the signs of weakness setting in, they pounce. They push the man who came up from the depths toward an evil act, a minor one. And if he takes the bait, he's theirs. He tastes the thrill and he is hooked. And now he lacks the strength to break away and make it down into the depths again.

Youth: That's very sad. I think it's true the good have depths of soul the evil lack.

Director: But maybe we've been wrong to say the evil are not deep.

Youth: How so?

Director: Can't someone evil hold a grudge? And might this grudge not run a long way down?

Youth: That's true.

Director: And speaking generally, do you believe the depths of pure and blackest hatred ever can be plumbed?

Youth: No, I would say they can be infinite.

Director: So if it's true the evil can be deep, how do they differ from the good?

Youth: The difference lies in what they hold, or don't.

Director: Now is it fair to say our acts will follow from the things we hold?

Youth: Of course.

Director: Then there are good and evil acts, accordingly?

Youth: No doubt.

Director: The actions of the ones who hold good things are always good?

Youth: Not always, no. It's possible to act against your character, against the things you hold.

Director: But that can't be the rule?

Youth: That's right. Because if it's the rule your character will change.

Director: Then character is more than just the values that you hold? It's also what you do?

Youth: It is.

Director: But should we take things further, Youth?

Youth: What do you mean?

Director: Should we declare that you hold values only when you act on them, that that's the test?

Youth: I think we should. It's easy to believe in something when you do not have to act on your belief.

Director: We have to put the values that we think we hold into the crucible of action, then we'll see how they turn out?

Youth: I think that's best.

Director: So character is what you do.

Youth: Agreed.

Director: And what you do takes strength?

Youth: Of course it does. The greater strength it takes, the stronger is your character.

Director: So you can train your character by taking on some actions that are difficult?

Youth: You can.

Director: Do you go looking for these things, or do you merely let them come to you?

Youth: I guess you look for them.

Father: You look for trouble, then?

Youth: Not everything that's difficult is trouble, Dad. It might be hard to lend support to someone that you love.

Father: I take your point. But does your character grow weak if you don't take on actions that are hard?

Youth: I think it does.

Father: So you will always take the harder road?

Youth: Not always, no. You need a break from time to time.

Father: But harder tasks will be the rule?

Youth: That's right. Or don't you think that I should have strong character?

Father: Of course I want for you to have strong character. I only fear the price.

Director: What price is that?

Father: The price that everyone must pay who takes the harder road. It takes a fair amount of agony to strengthen up a character.

Director: That's what you'll find upon the harder road?

Father: More often than you will on any other path.

Director: I don't believe that's true.

Father: But surely you've had agony along the way.

Director: I've had my share of difficulties, yes. But agony? What do you think that is?

Father: It's suffering at high intensity.

Director: What makes for high intensity?

Father: The feeling that you're suffering alone.

Director: So many suffer in this world. How can we think we're suffering alone? Is it because you're acting on a value that's unique, a value that nobody shares with you?

Father: No value such as that exists.

Director: Perhaps it's the degree to which the value's held? Could someone be so strong in how he grips a value that he's all alone?

Father: I think that's more the thing.

Director: But if he weren't alone, his suffering would be much less?

Father: That's how it seems to me.

Director: You'd rather that he share his path than walk it all alone?

Father: Your character grows stronger when you walk it all alone.

Director: But is that really true? Suppose you climb a mountain with a guide. Are you not stronger for the climb, despite the help?

Father: Of course you are. But there's a paucity of guides in life.

Youth: But you two are my guides.

Father: While that is true, it's also true that life requires you to go a stretch alone, my son. That is the hardest thing that you can do. You want the strongest character, correct?

Youth: I do.

Father: Then you must learn to go alone. Oh, you can end your isolation once you've learned. But you will always know you're not afraid of solitude. That makes you strong.

Youth: Director, do you think that's how it is?

Director: Your father has a point.

Youth: But you don't think it's agony to go it on your own?

Director: I don't. It can be hard, and even scary, yes. But agony? Not that. That comes from other things.

Youth: What other things?

Director: I'm sure you can imagine, Youth. But I will tell you one. It's agony if you're not on your proper path in life.

Youth: But how am I to know my proper path?

Father: Just listen to your gut.

Youth: That's it?

Father: That's it.

Director: Now look at us with all our talk of agony. Let's not forget its opposite.

Youth: Euphoria?

Director: Well, I was thinking more of simple pleasure, Youth. Are you aware that pleasure helps to build up character?

Youth: How so?

Director: You know about the pleasure of a job well done?

Youth: I do.

Director: Then tell me what you'd feel if you lived up to your own character through thick and thin.

Youth: I'd feel much more than just the pleasure of a job well done. I'd feel the pleasure of a victory.

Director: And how would that affect your character?

Youth: I think that it would fix it firm, like baking clay with sun.

Director: That's very nice. But do you know what happens when you've baked your clay?

Youth: You lose your flexibility.

Director: That's right. I know it's just a metaphor, but still, you cannot let success destroy your suppleness concerning truth. It's happened more than once.

Youth: What happens if it does?

Director: You come to lean on formulaic acts derived from past success.

Youth: Instead of trusting to your gut.

Father: I'm glad you understand.

Youth: So how should pleasure help you with your character?

Director: It's just a nice reward, a good incentive for another go.

Youth: That's it?

Director: That's plenty, don't you think?

Youth: I don't think pleasure is enough. We also must have pride incenting us.

Director: Agreed, though we're aware that pride comes with a pleasure all its own.

Youth: A pleasure for the strong.

Director: Indeed. Or do you think it's possible for weak men to be proud?

Youth: I think that weak men can be proud in secret, yes. They often pride themselves on foolish things. They can indulge themselves because they don't let on to how they feel.

Director: And if they do let on?

Youth: Then everyone will laugh.

10

Director: And what effect does laughter have?

Youth: It makes the weak but proud ashamed — or worse.

Director: You mean that it might drive these men to evil, Youth?

Youth: I do, in time.

Director: Suppose these men indeed are driven on to evil. Do we know enough if we're aware of what has made them turn? Or do we need a way to know their evil characters, as well?

Youth: We need to know their characters. It doesn't really matter why they turned. The fact is that they did.

Director: So how are we to know their characters?

Youth: We'd know them from the values that they hold, or don't.

Director: Can we just ask them what they hold?

Youth: Of course we can't. They won't declare their values just like that.

Director: But why? Are they embarrassed?

Youth: No, it isn't that.

Director: What is it then?

Youth: I think it's prudence, actually.

Director: It's prudent not to let your evil values be well known? Why's that?

Youth: Because the good will turn on you.

Director: The banded good?

Youth: I take your point. But still, the evil know enough to hide their characters.

Director: Except when they are in control, as in a tyranny?

Youth: That might well be the closest evil men can come to letting on to what they really are. But even then they try to hide the truth.

Director: But why? The good don't band as readily as we might like. Or do they band as soon as evil shows its face?

Youth: We know that isn't true. The bullies show their faces every day at school and no one's stopping them.

Father: The bullies are just dunces. Evil men are something more.

Youth: What more?

Father: They're dark in soul. With this in mind, are all your bullies really evil, Youth, or just a bunch of ignoramuses?

Youth: They're ignoramuses, and evil, too. A bully punched me in the face for standing up for truth! If that's not evil, I don't know what is.

Director: Youth has a point. Do you contest the evil nature of these boys?

Father: Don't get me wrong. I think they're scum. But evil? No. They might be dim of wit but they're not dark.

Director: What does it take for someone to be dark?

Father: He hides the truth about his character.

Director: And is it hard to hide your character?

Father: You have to tell persuasive lies and keep them straight. Your average bully can't do that.

Youth: Of course he can.

Father: Persuasive lies?

Youth: Forget about the lies. Suppose the bully had a gun. Suppose he shot me, Dad. Would that not be an evil act, regardless of how light or dark his soul might be?

Father: Your average bully wouldn't go that far.

Youth: But how can you be certain?

Father: I've got long experience with bullies, Youth. They're cowardly.

Youth: You're saying that the evil aren't?

Father: I'm simply saying that you shouldn't underestimate an evil man.

Director: Now where is strength in all of this?

Youth: It's on the side of good.

Director: Can you say more?

Youth: It takes no strength to lie, to darken up your evil character. What's hard is telling truth, is living truth. What's hard is being bright, not dark.

Director: What's hard about the truth?

Youth: The truth is generally unpopular.

Director: The truth, or certain sorts of truth?

Youth: The certain sorts of truth.

Director: How many live these certain sorts?

Youth: At best? I'd say there's one in every ten.

Director: And when these knowers of the certain sorts of truth band up, they're equal to the other nine?

Youth: Well, in a way they're greater than the nine.

Director: And all these knowers, are they good?

Youth: If they live up to what they know, they are.

Director: And those who don't live up to what they know about these truths, could they be evil men? Or can't the evil know the type of truth you mean?

Youth: Let's say they can.

Director: Alright. Then tell me, Youth. With whom is truth, the truth that is unpopular, most strong? The evil or the good?

Youth: The truth is strongest with the ones who live the truth, and not with those who merely know.

Director: Now why would those who know not live?

Youth: They'd rather hide in their dark caves than step out in the light.

Director: They hate the light?

Youth: They do.

Director: Would it take strength to step out in the light?

Youth: I think that it would take a great amount of strength.

Director: But once you've lived with truth a while, then it gets easier?

Youth: I think that's true. But then you must move on to greater truths, and that is difficult.

Director: You must move on? Why can't you simply live beside your cave in peace?

Youth: Then you're not living up to your potential, right?

Director: It seems you have a point. But would you say that evil men have got potential, Youth?

Youth: Well, if they do, they don't live up to it.

Director: They squander their potential?

Youth: Yes.

Director: But still, they have their strength? Or do you think the evil can't be strong?

Youth: No, evil men are often strong. Just not in character.

Director: And character, and truth, and light are what bring happiness?

Youth: They are.

Director: The lack of all or any one of these brings misery?

Youth: That's what I like to think.

Director: But is it possible that any of these things — the truth, your character, or light — itself brings misery?

Youth: I can't see how.

Father: I think I can. Suppose that you believe that you are good at something, Youth. But then suppose that someone proves to you you're really not. The truth might make you miserable.

Youth: No, I would say that it's the lie you tell yourself that makes you miserable, and not the truth.

Director: The truth, is it a catalyst?

Youth: It is. It helps to drive away the false. And in the end, once you've accepted what is true, you'll find your proper happiness.

Director: Do you believe that everyone is good at something, Youth?

Youth: I do.

Director: So all you have to do is find that thing?

Youth: That's right.

Director: And just be good at it and live in truth and you will have your happiness?

Father: I think you also need some luck. You can be good at what you do, but if you're in an accident that leaves you so you cannot do your thing, can you have happiness?

Youth: Well, maybe happiness relies on some degree of luck. As long as nothing accidental interferes with what you want to do, I'd say that you can have your happiness.

Director: Now what about the things that are not accidents?

Youth: What kind of things?

Director: The things you bring upon yourself.

Youth: You mean mistakes?

Director: Let's call them that. Mistakes are things you do that lead to some degree, however small, of misery.

Youth: Mistakes can distance you from truth.

Director: Let's have a good example here.

Youth: You tell a friend you like a thing. The truth is that you don't.

Director: And this mistake would make you miserable?

Youth: I think it would to some degree.

Director: If you tell lots of lies like this, do you become an evil man?

Youth: Well, I don't know. It's possible to be in misery but still be good.

Father: But over time? What happens to a man who lives for long in misery? I think that he grows jealous of the ones who have their happiness. And jealousy can lead to evil deeds.

Director: But is this always so?

Youth: No, I believe that someone who is strong could live a long, long while in misery and never do an evil deed.

Director: Because he holds on tight to all the values of the good?

Youth: That's right.

Director: Except for truthfulness?

Youth: He only is untrue about himself and how he feels.

Director: What are the other values of the good?

Youth: I'd say there's courage and there's loyalty. There's fairness and there's moderation, too.

Father: I don't believe that he can hold those other values, Youth. His lies have started him upon a downward slide. The misery he feels from all his little lies will make him lie all that much more.

Director: What happens then?

Father: I think his loyalty will slip. For how can he be loyal if he isn't honest anymore? The bond of loyalty is truth.

Director: What's next?

Father: His courage goes. When you're surrounded by your lies, and are no longer loyal to your friends, what moral fiber do you have to stand up tall?

Director: And then?

Father: Your jealousy of upright souls will make you be unfair, to satisfy your spite. And here the seeds of misery are truly sown. You'll start to hate yourself. And when you do you won't be moderate. For misery and moderation can't walk hand in hand for long. The miserable indulge themselves in order to obtain relief, however fleetingly.

Director: And that's the end of it, this downward slide?

Father: Imprudence is the final phase. When you are truly miserable you make mistakes with regularity — and they are some mistakes. You've gotten to the point where you can't help yourself. You've reached the end.

Director: And are you evil then?

Father: You have abandoned all the values of the good. What do you think you are?

Youth: It doesn't have to be that way. It's as I said. You can be good and miserable at once.

Director: Do you have friends who're good and miserable?

Youth: I do.

Director: And do they lie to you?

Youth: They sometimes do.

Director: About the things they like?

Youth: That's right. They'll say that they're enjoying something when I know they're not.

Director: Why do you think they lie?

Youth: I wish I knew.

Director: But do you lie to them?

Youth: I don't.

Father: But why have friends you know are lying to you, Youth?

Youth: The lies they tell don't harm me, Dad.

Father: But lies, whatever sort of lies, will put them on the downward slide.

Youth: I'll watch for that.

Director: Suppose they don't begin the downward slide but grow more miserable with every passing year. Would you still like to have them as your friends?

Youth: Well, I'd be loyal to them, right?

Director: And in your loyalty would you attempt to bring these friends to happiness?

Youth: Of course.

Director: And would this happiness derive from speaking truth about the way they feel?

Youth: I think it would — or rather, that would be the way to start.

Director: So you'd encourage them to speak the truth.

Youth: I would, most certainly.

Father: And if they never do? Won't they begin to pull you down into their misery? The prudent thing must be to limit your exposure to these friends.

Youth: But prudence can be cold.

Father: As cold as empty loyalty, as loyalty that isn't based on truth? If there's no truth, what loyalty is there?

Youth: But they tell truth — just not about themselves and how they feel.

Director: You mean that they tell other truths, at times important truths?

Youth: That's right.

Father: Which truth is more important to a friendship, Youth? The truth about yourself or something else, some other truth?

Youth: I guess we have to say that it's the truth about yourself.

Father: And if a friend will lie about himself not once but many, many times — what does this mean?

Youth: It means we're forced to say the friendship can't be very good.

11

Director: When people lie about themselves, about the things they like, do they feel good?

Youth: No, I don't think they do.

Director: And if they don't feel good, do you believe their spirits would be low?

Youth: I do.

Director: What would it take to lift their spirits up?

Youth: I think they'd have to turn to something they enjoy.

Director: What sorts of things might they enjoy?

Youth: Oh, I don't know. It could be anything.

Director: Is truth a thing they might enjoy?

Youth: That sounds a little weird.

Director: You mean to say you don't enjoy the truth?

Youth: The truth is not about enjoyment. It's about . . . the truth!

Director: But when you line yourself right up with truth, don't you feel good?

Youth: Of course I do.

Director: Don't you enjoy yourself when you feel good?

Youth: I guess you're right. Let's say I do enjoy the truth.

Director: And would you say that you enjoy it more than anything?

Youth: I would. At least when I live up to it.

Director: And it takes strength to live up to the truth?

Youth: It does — a great amount.

Director: Your friends who're good and miserable, do you believe they have this strength?

Youth: I think they do for certain things.

Director: But if they were completely weak? Could they live up to any truth?

Youth: You mean if they were weak in soul? They couldn't, no.

Director: And those who live up to the truth, you'd say that they are good?

Youth: I would.

Director: And is the truth the only way of being good?

Youth: It is.

Director: And everyone who isn't good is evil? Or can you be neither, Youth? In other words, can you be in-between?

Youth: Let's say it's either–or.

Director: Then does this mean that those who're weak in soul are evil since they can't live up to truth?

Youth: I guess it does.

Director: Alright. But now I'm wondering. If you are strong in soul, must you be good by some necessity?

Youth: No, evil men are sometimes very strong. They simply have an evil soul.

Director: But then that means that they're not strong in truth?

Youth: That's right. The evil ones deny the truth. They don't have any moral worth.

Director: And moral worth is closeness to the truth in how you live your life?

Youth: Exactly, yes.

Director: The closer to the truth you live, the greater is your worth?

Youth: That's right.

Director: But what about the truth of evil, Youth?

Youth: What do you mean?

Director: I mean, the fact that certain evil people hate the good, the people who are good, is just exactly that — a fact. And they live up to it. So aren't they living close to truth?

Youth: However that might be, the evil are at distance from the greater truth.

Director: The greater truth? What's that?

Youth: The moral truth.

Director: That justice rules the universe?

Youth: I think you're making fun of me.

Director: Oh no, I'm not. Do you believe that justice rules the universe?

Youth: Essentially I do, although at times I have my doubts.

Director: And if the good align with that, with justice, Youth, they too will rule?

Youth: Will rule the universe? That sounds absurd.

Director: But isn't that exactly what's at stake?

Youth: In truth? It is.

Director: The battle for the universe. Or is it that? If justice always wins, what sort of battle could it be?

Youth: Well, maybe justice only wins if all the good align with it.

Director: You mean the evil might just win?

Youth: That's right. It's possible injustice wins.

Director: And if injustice wins, so too the false will win?

Youth: It will.

Director: Do you believe that all that's just is true?

Youth: I do.

Director: And do you think that all that's true is just?

Youth: Ideally, yes — when dealing with the moral truth.

Director: So if the good are true along these lines they're doing what it takes to win?

Youth: They are. They have to come to know the truth and live in justice, yes.

Director: This truth they have to learn, what is it, Youth?

Youth: They have to learn the truth of everything.

Director: Of everything?

Youth: The good must be quite strong.

Director: But out of everything, where do the good begin?

Youth: They start at home — themselves.

Director: And then?

Youth: The people close to them.

Director: Are people our sole concern? Or do we care about the physics and the chemistry of things — of matter?

Youth: Yes, we do. But that is secondary.

Director: People are what count. Indeed. But don't you think that there's a physics and a chemistry to people, Youth, the way they interact? Or is it foolish to believe there is?

Youth: No, I don't think it's foolish.

Director: Then we'll learn the truth about the individuals we know. And then we'll learn the truth about the way they interact.

Youth: That's right. And when we do we can be one with truth.

Director: And truth will make us strong? But doesn't it take strength to learn the truth?

Youth: It does. You need the seed before you get the tree.

Director: And all of us have got the seed?

Youth: I think that's so, the good and evil both. But evil men don't nurture truth.

Director: What happens to their seeds?

Youth: They're cast on barren ground and lost.

Father: When does this happen, typically? When they are very young?

Youth: It doesn't really matter when.

Director: So what if someone nurtures truth and starts to grow a tree?

Youth: He has to take good care or else the tree will die.

Director: Then it's not given that you'll always be at one with truth because you grew a tree? The tree can always die?

Youth: That's right.

Director: And it takes strength to take good care and keep the tree alive?

Youth: It does. But trees of truth give strength in turn.

Director: I see. It all works out. But are we sure the evil never nurture truth, not even secretly?

Youth: The evil are not nurturers.

Director: Suppose they foster truth they know about the good, the ones we think are good.

Youth: Like what?

Director: Like whether they are hypocrites.

Youth: You mean the ones who only act like they are good?

Director: The same.

Youth: You think the evil do a favor to the good, the truly good? They point out hypocrites? While that may be, the truly good should know a hypocrite quite easily.

Director: If they all know a hypocrite for what he is, then why are there so many hypocrites around? Or am I wrong and there are only few?

Youth: No, I believe you're right. I can't explain the reason why so many hypocrites exist.

Director: But those who're truly good won't tolerate a hypocrite? What do they do, just banish him?

Youth: They call him what he is, for all to know, and that should be enough.

Director: Does it take strength to be a hypocrite?

Youth: I can't see how.

Director: So hypocrites are weak?

Youth: They are.

Director: And are they evil men?

Youth: Of course.

Director: Do you know evil hypocrites?

Youth: I do, at school.

Director: Are they the students or the teachers?

Youth: Both.

Director: What's worse, a student or a teacher as a hypocrite?

Youth: A teacher is.

Director: Can you say why?

Youth: Because he has authority.

Director: Authority makes every little problem worse?

Youth: Hypocrisy is not a little thing.

Director: Why not?

Youth: Why not? Because it isn't fair! The teacher tells us what to do.

Director: You mean the teacher preaches values that he doesn't hold?

Youth: Exactly so.

Director: He says he values truthfulness, but he tells lies?

Youth: That's right.

Director: It makes you feel indignant, no?

Youth: It does.

Director: You want to punish him for telling lies while preaching truthfulness?

Youth: I do.

Director: But what if he told lies but didn't preach?

Youth: You mean if he were not a hypocrite but just a simple liar?

Director: Yes.

Youth: But teachers are supposed to serve as models to the young.

Director: So he's a hypocrite by virtue of his role?

Youth: I think he is.

Director: Authorities should always serve as models to the young?

Youth: They should.

Director: So they are hypocrites, of sorts, whenever they are less than good?

Youth: Agreed.

Director: And if a person who tells lies is no authority, and doesn't preach about the value of the truth, he's just a simple liar, right, and not a hypocrite?

Youth: That's right.

Director: Hypocrisy is something worse atop the basic, underlying vice?

Youth: It is.

Director: And it takes strength to practice what you preach?

Youth: Of course it does.

Director: But does such practice also give you strength?

Youth: It gives you moral strength.

Director: The strength it takes is nothing to the strength it gives?

Youth: That's right. The strength it takes is just a little water on the seed of moral strength.

Director: And when the seed of moral strength has grown into a tree the sun and rain take care of it, no effort on your part?

Youth: That's where the metaphor falls short. You must take care of it yourself, as we have said. The tree can always die.

Director: It is a constant effort, then?

Youth: It is. But you grow stronger than the effort you put in.

Director: A wise investment, Youth. But how does moral strength compare to simple strength?

Youth: You mean the strength of evil men?

Director: I mean the strength of anyone. Before your moral tree has grown, you just have simple strength, correct?

Youth: I guess.

Director: So tell me how your simple strength compares to moral strength.

Youth: I'd like to say your moral strength is stronger than your simple strength.

Director: And why is that?

Youth: Your moral strength builds up the fiber of your soul.

Director: And simple strength does not?

Youth: That's right.

Director: The soul, is it essentially a moral thing?

Youth: I think it is.

Director: And soul's the soil where the moral trees can grow?

Youth: It is.

Director: What happens if we farm our souls?

Youth: I don't know what you mean.

Director: I mean, suppose that we plant trees that bear sweet fruit. Can we not gather in this fruit?

Youth: I guess.

Director: Then we can sell the fruit?

Youth: I don't like how that sounds.

Director: But why?

Youth: Our virtue shouldn't be for sale.

Director: Oh, not our virtue, Youth — the fruits of it.

Youth: Well, maybe then.

Director: But you don't like the notion, still.

Youth: I don't.

Director: And that's because your virtue is a sacred thing?

Youth: I think you're mocking me again.

Director: I'm not. I want to know why we can't sell the fruits.

Youth: Because our virtue then is mercenary.

Director: Ah, I see the problem now. Our virtue must be pure. It's virtue for the sake of virtue, right, and not the things it brings?

Youth: That's right.

Director: But doesn't virtue bring us friends?

Youth: It does. But that is only natural.

Director: In other words, there is no sale of virtue's fruits?

Youth: Correct, and that's because our friendships are the fruits themselves.

Director: It seems I had it wrong. What other fruit is there?

12

Youth: What other fruits of virtue do we have? I'd say that we have peace, and happiness.

Director: But didn't we agree that happiness takes some degree of luck?

Youth: That's right, we did.

Director: And what of peace? Does it take luck?

Youth: I think there's inner peace and outer peace. The inner peace is up to you. The outer peace depends, to some degree, on luck.

Director: But if your outer peace is bad — in other words, you have no peace — can you have inner peace?

Youth: I think it takes an act of will, but yes.

Director: So inner peace depends on virtue, then?

Youth: That's right. And so the evil have no inner peace.

Director: At any time?

Youth: At any time.

Director: Do they believe the good have peace?

Youth: I'm sure they do. That makes them hate the good all that much more.

Director: But if they know the good have peace, do they not want that peace themselves?

Youth: I think they want it more than anything.

Director: Is that because you think the evil are tormented? Justice once again?

Youth: You don't think that the evil long for peace?

Director: Well, let's suppose they do. Why don't they ever come to it?

Youth: I think they're lost.

Director: Lost souls? They don't know how to find their way? If that's the case, could we not show them where it is? Could we not speak the truth to them?

Youth: We could, but they won't listen to a word we say. They are too arrogant.

Director: They'd rather keep their arrogance than have a chance at lasting peace?

Youth: If it were just the arrogance perhaps they'd have a chance. But there is more to it than that. They will not do the things the good must do in order to be good, in order to have inner peace.

Director: You mean they can't control their wicked urges, Youth? You mean they lie, and cheat, and steal?

Youth: That is exactly what I mean.

Director: And virtue is the only way to inner peace?

Youth: That's right.

Director: Then virtue takes priority above all else?

Youth: Of course it does.

Director: And this is how it is for all the good?

Youth: It is.

Director: Now what if virtue comes in conflict with a friend?

Youth: You mean the friend would have me do a thing that isn't virtuous? Why, I'd choose virtue, naturally.

Director: But what about your loyalty?

Youth: All loyalty must be to virtue first.

Director: And that's because your friends derive from virtue, are the fruits of virtue, right?

Youth: That's how it is.

Director: Do you have friends you wouldn't say are simply good?

Youth: You mean that they're not perfect? Yes, of course I do. They don't conflict with virtue, though.

Director: So they're not evil, right?

Youth: That's right. They do not always put their virtue first, but they're not bad.

Director: They're somewhere in between the two extremes of perfect good and perfect evil, then?

Youth: I guess.

Director: And sometimes they put virtue first.

Youth: They do.

Director: Now when do they do that?

Youth: When it's not very difficult.

Director: But isn't when it's difficult exactly when it counts?

Youth: What can I say? Should I abandon them as friends because they are not simply good?

Director: I'm not proposing that. But tell me, Youth, about your friends who are indeed among the simply good.

Youth: Well . . . I don't have such friends.

Director: The good are rarer than we thought! But tell me this. Are you among the simply good?

Youth: I'd like to think I am. But no, I'm not.

Director: And why is that?

Youth: Because I'm human and I make mistakes.

Director: Do you believe that anyone is simply good?

Youth: To tell the truth, I don't. The goodness that we've spoken of is something that we strive towards.

Director: But evil men don't strive.

Youth: They most assuredly do not.

Director: So can we say that those who strive are good?

Youth: I think we can.

Director: And we can say the good aren't perfect. If they were they wouldn't have to strive.

Youth: That's true.

Director: What does it mean to strive?

Youth: To try your best.

Director: Does it take strength to strive?

Youth: It takes a great amount.

Director: And why is that?

Youth: Because the virtue that you want to live is hard.

Director: Would it be easier to slide into an evil state?

Youth: Much easier by far.

Director: What's hard about the virtues, Youth?

Youth: They take a great amount of discipline.

Director: Is discipline unpleasant, then?

Youth: It's only pleasant once you've mastered it.

Director: But still you have to strive? Does it get better as you go?

Youth: You mean does it get easier? It's as we said with truth.

Director: You mean you're always moving on to harder things? You don't seem very comfortable when things get easier.

Youth: Why should I be? Your virtue is a thing you have to earn. What good is it if it is something that you simply have, or have it easy with?

Director: I think I see what you are saying here. You do not want to say that virtue is unpleasant, right? But you don't want to say it's easy to obtain. And once obtained, you do not want to say it's easy to maintain. What good is it if it is easy to obtain, or easy to maintain?

Youth: Precisely that.

Director: But what if virtue is a gift?

Youth: A gift? You mean it's not deserved?

Director: Suppose a person finds it very easy not to lie, or cheat, or steal. Suppose it isn't through an effort of the will. Suppose it just comes naturally. This person surely counts among the virtuous. Or wouldn't you agree?

Youth: I guess I would. But I'm not sure it's possible for virtue to be easy in that way. We all have times when it would be much easier to lie.

Director: But I'm not sure that all of us would find it easier. Suppose you have a conscience that would torture you because of lies you've told. Would it be easier to lie or tell the truth?

Youth: I take your point.

Director: And what of conscience, Youth? Are we so sure that it consists of all the lines we've drawn, as we have said?

Youth: I think it does.

Director: But what if conscience, too, is really just a gift?

Youth: I don't like where we're headed here.

Director: You want to earn your virtue, right? You wouldn't have it as a gift?

Youth: That's right.

Director: You want to earn the conscience that ensures your virtue, too?

Youth: I wouldn't have it as a gift.

Director: You wouldn't have a single thing about you as a gift?

Youth: I wouldn't go that far.

Director: Because your body and your mind, their soundness and their level of ability, are gifts?

Youth: They are. But they aren't moral things.

Director: The moral must be earned?

Youth: It must.

Director: So we must strive for moral things?

Youth: That's how it is.

Director: Is it the sort of striving that we do to win a race against our fellow men?

Youth: I think it's striving with yourself.

Director: To be as good as you can be?

Youth: Just so.

Director: And who will judge this striving with yourself?

Youth: Well, I will be the judge — and so will all my fellow men.

Director: They'll judge you by results?

Youth: They will.

Director: The evil men will judge you, too?

Youth: It's as we've said — the evil make a study of the good. They know enough to know an honest man when one appears.

Director: You really would submit yourself to judgment by an evil man?

Youth: Well, there's the risk that he would lie and say that I'm not virtuous. But in his heart, his rotten heart, I think he'd know the truth.

Director: A man that's good is recognized by everyone?

Youth: He is.

Director: But no one knows how much the man has had to strive to be that way, except for him?

Youth: The others who are striving would have some idea.

Director: But what if he is striving to new heights?

Youth: Then no one knows exactly what he's had to do except for him.

Director: Do you aspire to the heights?

Youth: I do.

Director: And could you stand it if you're all alone?

Youth: I think I could.

Director: Are you alone right now?

Youth: Of course I'm not. I'm here with you and Dad.

Director: And you believe that we both strive?

Youth: I know you do.

Director: When you're at school, are you alone?

Youth: I don't think anybody cares for virtue like I do.

Father: Perhaps that is your gift.

Youth: Perhaps it is my curse.

Director: How do you know that no one cares like you? You've tried to talk to everyone?

Youth: Well, no.

Director: Then why do you presume to know? Perhaps you need to search out virtue in your peers. Is there a boy who doesn't lie that much?

Youth: There is.

Director: What if you start with him, and ask him why he doesn't lie?

Youth: You think that's all I need to do, just ask him why he doesn't lie?

Director: That isn't all. But that might be the way you start.

Youth: What then?

Director: You might just talk about the truth and all the virtues, Youth.

Youth: Alright. I'll try on Monday when I'm back in school. But let's suppose he doesn't care for virtue, that he doesn't have the gift. What then?

Director: Well, are there others who appear to value truth?

Youth: There are.

Director: Then talk to them.

Youth: But what if they don't care the way I do?

Father: Your gift is all that much more precious, then.

Youth: But what am I to do with it?

Father: Just trust your gut, my boy, and you'll know what to do when it is time.

13

Director: Now, Father, it at times appears to me that gut, in large part anyway, is just a gift. Do you agree?

Father: In large part, yes. But don't forget we said we'd feed the gut with good, slow reasonings.

Director: Of course. And so this means we earn a part of gut, however small?

Father: It does.

Director: Do you believe that evil men can feed their guts with reasonings?

Father: With evil reasonings, they can.

Director: And when they listen to their guts, their guts can make them strong in evil, right? Just like the way when men of virtue listen to their guts they make them strong in good?

Father: That's how it is.

Director: And so it's bad for evil men to listen to their guts?

Father: That's true.

Director: They ought to listen to the reasonings of those who're good?

Father: They ought to, anyway.

Director: Instead they try to reason with the good?

Father: Of course they do. The Devil has a silver tongue.

Director: So how does he persuade?

Father: He offers up the easy answer, right?

Youth: But don't the good know better?

Father: Yes, they do — right in their guts.

Director: And so the evil try to get them off their guts with promises of ease?

Father: That's right.

Director: What sort of man would sacrifice his proper good for ease?

Father: A weak man would.

Director: So then it all comes down to strength?

Father: It does.

Director: Do you believe the evil ever really listen to the good?

Father: The evil want the easy way. The way of good is never easy, right?

Director: That seems correct. And so the good can't reason with the evil, then?

Father: That's absolutely true.

Director: Is everyone who hopes to take the easy way an evil man?

Father: That sounds a little harsh. The lazy are not evil, necessarily.

Director: But we are sure the good must try, must strive?

Father: We are.

Director: Now please remind us, Youth, of what they strive toward.

Youth: The truth, to know and live the truth.

Director: What does it mean to live the truth?

Youth: You hold yourself accountable to it.

Director: You do this all alone?

Youth: It's good to have the help of friends.

Director: Who also hold themselves accountable to truth?

Youth: That's right.

Director: What if opinions vary as to what is true?

Youth: Well, that would be unfortunate.

Director: Indeed. But what are you to do if that's the case?

Youth: I guess you have to listen to your gut.

Director: And go your separate ways?

Youth: That might be why the good don't band that readily.

Director: You might be right. But if that's so, then what would make them band?

Youth: Agreement on the truth of evil's threat.

Director: Of evil's threat to those who're good?

Youth: Of course.

Director: What makes the truth of evil's threat more clear than that of other truths?

Youth: The element of fear.

Director: The element of fear? What does this fear accomplish in the mind?

Youth: It helps to focus things.

Director: And there's no fear about the other truths?

Youth: No, I don't think there is. It's evil that one fears.

Director: So there's no focus on the other things?

Youth: There is. But you must focus on your own, without the aid of fear.

Director: And what incentive do you have to focus on the true, without the aid of fear?

Youth: The true will bring you happiness.

Director: And that is that?

Youth: It is.

Director: But truth is not the easy way, and that is why not everyone adheres to it?

Youth: That's right.

Director: They trade their happiness for ease?

Youth: They do.

Director: But can they know that this is what they do?

Youth: I think they do.

Director: Does that make sense? I mean, if happiness is in their reach then why not go for it? I wonder if they are confused. They might not know that happiness is possible.

Youth: You mean they might not know they're strong enough for it?

Director: I do. Perhaps they need to learn what's possible for them.

Youth: And who will teach them that?

Director: Why, you and I, my friend.

Youth: But certain people are not teachable.

Director: The evil, right? What makes them evil, Youth?

Youth: They've formed their wills on evil ends.

Director: And they pursue these ends instead of what it takes for happiness?

Youth: They do. And it's a shame because a number of them could be strong enough for happiness.

Director: It's funny you should mention shame. Are they ashamed they've traded truth for ease?

Youth: No, I don't think they are. But if they are, their hate drowns out the shame.

Director: They hate the ones who love the truth?

Youth: They do.

Director: But why?

Youth: Because they make the evil ones look bad.

Director: But in whose eyes?

Youth: Why, even in the evils' own.

Director: The evil lack a certain self-respect?

Youth: Of course they do.

Director: Can anything be done to bring them to the truth?

Youth: You'd have to drive them with a whip.

Director: The virtuous would use this whip?

Youth: They would — with zeal.

Director: With zeal? Because they love the truth?

Youth: Because of all the hate they've had to bear.

Director: They take revenge by driving evil men toward truth?

Youth: And that's ironic, no?

Director: But why ironic, Youth?

Youth: They're doing them a favor. Truth will set the evil free.

Director: But is that what they want?

Youth: Who cares? It's what is best for them.

Director: Who knows what's best for whom?

Youth: The virtuous know what is best for evil men.

Director: How do they know?

Youth: They're guided by the truth.

Director: And if they'd know the truth about the lives of others, first they'd have to know the truth about their own?

Youth: That's right — or otherwise they would be hypocrites.

Director: You say the truth will set the evil free. But when exactly are they freed?

Youth: When they no longer need the whip.

Director: When they take up the truth all on their own?

Youth: Exactly so.

Director: But what if they don't take it up? The virtuous just keep on whipping them?

Youth: I guess.

Director: Then that becomes their full time job?

Youth: This isn't sounding very good.

Director: But why? Because revenge no longer seems so sweet?

Youth: Well, they would be consumed by their revenge. That can't be good.

Director: Perhaps we should forget about the whip. It might be best, instead, to spend our energies on those who truly seem to want but do not have the truth.

Youth: That sounds much better, yes. What do we need to do to help them out?

Director: Well, first we need to know if they are strong enough to listen to the truth. You do think it takes strength to really listen, right?

Youth: I do. It takes the strength of honesty, of being honest with yourself.

Director: Do truth and honesty go hand in hand?

Youth: They do.

Director: If you don't have the truth, is being honest with yourself of any use?

Youth: Of course it's not.

Director: And what about the other way?

Youth: You mean you have the truth but are not honest with yourself? No, that's no good.

Director: Is that the way the evil are when they have truth?

Youth: It is.

Director: So why should we bring truth to people who show no capacity for being honest with themselves?

Youth: Well, I don't think we should.

Director: But let's suppose we've got our listener, a man with strength in inner honesty — and he wants truth. Does it take strength to tell this man the truth?

Youth: I think it does.

Director: But what is easier than speaking truth to such a man, to one who wants in all his honesty to know? You'd think the words would fly right off our lips.

Youth: But it takes more than inner honesty for us to trust this man with truth. He has to show an outer honesty as well.

Director: We must be strong enough to see if he is truly honest in and out? And then we must be strong enough to trust? What does it take to trust?

Youth: It takes a knowledge of the person's character.

Director: The values that he holds?

Youth: That's right.

Director: And how do we obtain a knowledge of the values that he holds?

Youth: We have to talk to him, and watch the way he acts.

Director: To see if what he says and does are one?

Youth: That's right.

Director: And if they're not?

Youth: We have to question what he's telling us.

Director: Because he is a hypocrite?

Youth: Of course.

Director: But here's the troubling thing. It's possible a hypocrite can tell us truth.

Youth: However that may be, I wouldn't trust the man.

Director: Yet trust and truth are different things. If someone evil tells you truth, would you reject it out of hand?

Youth: You mean it's really true? I guess I'd listen. But I'd get away from him as soon as possible.

Director: How would you know it's true?

Youth: I'd have to listen to my gut.

Director: Suppose he speaks persuasively of something that is false. And then suppose that in your gut you feel it's true.

Father: You mean he makes you feel that something's good that really isn't good?

Director: For instance, yes. What then?

Youth: When dealing with a man like this you still must listen to your gut. But then you have to verify.

14

Director: So you can't always simply trust your gut?

Youth: I guess you can't — not gut alone, at any rate. I mean, suppose that someone speaks the truth but in your gut you feel it's false. What then?

Director: Then what's the use of gut?

Youth: It's useful when you haven't got the time to verify. You take your chances then.

Director: And do you take your chances when it's simply hard to verify a thing?

Youth: I think that many do.

Director: So gut can be a crutch when something's hard to verify, when you don't really want to do what must be done to learn the truth?

Youth: It can.

Director: What do you use to verify the truth of what is said?

Youth: Your mind?

Director: Please tell us how your mind is different than your gut.

Youth: Your gut is feel. Your mind is rational.

Director: And truth is always rational?

Youth: I'm not so sure. I think at times the truth is feel.

Director: Then do you listen to your mind or gut?

Youth: Well, both.

Director: Then truth is when your mind and gut agree?

Youth: I think it is.

Director: When mind and gut agree, they're strong?

Youth: They are.

Director: Because the truth is strong and they're aligned with it?

Youth: That's right.

Director: But can the mind alone discover truth?

Youth: Not if it isn't tied to gut.

Director: And just the same, the gut alone cannot discover truth?

Youth: I think that's right.

Director: Then why do we believe we ought to trust our gut?

Youth: Because we know the dangers of the mind alone.

Director: What are those dangers, Youth?

Youth: The mind can over-simplify.

Director: What does that mean?

Youth: It's like in physics, when you don't account for friction. There's a lot like that in life.

Director: The gut brings home reality to mind?

Youth: It does.

Director: But then again, the mind brings home reality to gut?

Youth: I think that's true — as far as truth is rational.

Director: Is gut, is feel, irrational?

Youth: Well, there are reasons for the way we feel. And we have said that we can reason to our gut. So I don't think it's right to say that gut is just irrational.

Director: The gut is mixed? And what about the mind? Is it not mixed as well? Or are we all completely rational in mind?

Youth: No, I would say the mind is mixed.

Director: Now what about your heart and soul, my friend? Are they irrational or rational or both?

Youth: I think they, too, are mixed. But I don't see the point of focusing on this. What really counts is truth. As long as it is truth it doesn't matter how we got to it, through means irrational or rational.

Director: And those who get to truth are strong?

Youth: Of course.

Director: Suppose we have to swim against the tide to get to truth.

Youth: Well, that takes strength.

Father: But what exactly is the tide?

Youth: It's what is popular.

Father: So it takes strength to be unpopular.

Youth: It does.

Father: But can't the tide itself be true?

Youth: Of course it can. That's when you let it carry you along.

Director: Suppose the tide is one of truth for quite a long, long time. What happens to the ones who simply go with it, who let it carry them along? Will they be strong enough to fight the tide if it should ever turn? Or are they weak from merely drifting all the time?

Youth: I think they're weak. But here's the thing. The tide must always turn. It's in the law of things.

Director: So you believe that no one has it easy, then? We all must swim against the tide at times?

Youth: We must.

Director: And that's because the universe is fair? There's equal hardship for us all?

Youth: I wouldn't go that far.

Director: But if there isn't equal hardship, some of us have got it easier?

Youth: That's fair to say.

Director: And aren't there ones who simply go along with every tide they can, regardless of how true it is?

Youth: There are.

Director: Do they develop equal strength to those who often swim against the tide?

Youth: Of course they don't.

Director: Adversity develops strength?

Youth: That's right.

Director: But if you want to grow as strong as possible, should you just always swim against the flow, regardless of its quality?

Youth: You'd swim against the true? But only evil men do that. No, you must rest at times. That gives your swimming muscles time to grow. If you are always at it you will wear yourself right down. You'll lose your strength.

Director: A point well made. But tell me this. Are there more evil tides than good? In other words, do good men get but little rest?

Youth: I think that's true.

Director: What makes this so?

Youth: So many people settle for the false, and this creates the evil tide.

Director: Are those who settle evil, Youth?

Youth: I think they are.

Director: Perhaps we ought to make a clear distinction here. Now, there are those who simply go along with evil, yes?

Youth: Agreed.

Director: They're passive, right?

Youth: They are.

Director: But there are also those who actively attack the good?

Youth: That's true.

Director: Does it much matter which of these two sorts a person is?

Youth: No, I don't think it does. They're equally as bad, as far as I'm concerned.

Director: And should we treat them both the same?

Youth: Why shouldn't we?

Father: Because it might be possible to stir the passive up and make them active in the truth.

Youth: But if we stir them up it's likely they'll lash out at us.

Director: Is that a risk that we should take?

Youth: The odds of our success are very long. We need to have a way of knowing who is likely to take up with truth. We can't just stir up every hornet's nest.

Director: So where should we begin?

Youth: Well, first, I think we have to find the ones who didn't settle out of laziness.

Director: You mean we find the ones who simply didn't know it's possible to live the truth?

Youth: I do.

Director: What does it take to educate their souls?

Youth: We need to offer them the spark of truth.

Director: And then they'll blaze? What happens with the ones who don't?

Youth: Some are afraid and put the fire out whenever it starts up.

Director: Afraid of what? The truth?

Youth: I think that many are afraid of truth.

Director: But what about the truth is bad?

Youth: It makes you question your beliefs.

Father: But that is good, if you would have belief that's true.

Youth: For us, it is. But not for everyone.

Director: It's better, then, for them to live a lie?

Youth: That's what a number of the passive ones believe.

Director: But do they really know their life's a lie?

Youth: I think that many of them do.

Director: But tell me then, what happens to the passive ones that we're successful with, the ones who actively begin to question what they know?

Youth: They sift through what they think they know and lose the false.

Director: They keep the true and live that truth, and that is how they blaze?

Youth: That's right.

Director: And what's the hardest thing they'll have to do?

Youth: I'd say that it's the letting go of what is false.

Director: Why can't they just let go?

Youth: Because they used their false beliefs to navigate their way through life. It takes some time to learn the use of truth, to get their bearings straight. They clutch the false until they do. And then they have to trust in truth enough to finally let go. This all is very hard.

Director: I see. But can you give a good example, Youth?

Youth: There is a boy at school who thought he should be everybody's friend. He came around, through talks with me, and saw that this is false. But now he's lost. He has to work out where he is, and how to act.

Director: So you can know the truth, but acting on the truth is quite another thing?

Youth: Exactly so. You have to know it first, and then you have to learn to act.

Director: Suppose you act the truth but do not know that it's the truth.

Youth: I'm not sure that is possible.

Director: Suppose you simply listen to your gut and act accordingly, and this aligns with truth. Could you not only learn much later that your gut is true?

Youth: I guess.

Director: And isn't it the same with those who act the false but do not know it's false? In either case there's ignorance.

Youth: That's true.

Director: Suppose we only have a limited amount of time. Which of these two should we approach in hopes of shedding light?

Youth: The ones who act the truth.

Director: And why is that?

Youth: At least they've got their guts. And that gives us a starting place.

Director: Now, would you say that gut's a sort of inner eye?

Youth: I would.

Director: And mind can also be an eye?

Youth: That's right. We need both eyes to see.

Director: The mind can verify the gut, and gut can verify the mind? So once a person sees with both his eyes he knows the truth?

Youth: Agreed.

Director: Now, how do we get those who only see the truth with gut to open up their minds?

Youth: We take the truth within their guts and show them how it feels for mind to be in harmony with it.

Director: We teach them not to fear the mind?

Youth: Exactly, yes.

Director: But do these people just have truth, and only truth, within their guts?

Youth: No, they'll have what is false as well. I don't know if it's possible to have a gut that's simply pure in truth.

Director: So what of all the false?

Youth: I don't think we can tackle it until we've worked a good long while with truth. They need to learn to trust the mind. And once they do, we find a little thing within their gut that's false and show them what it really is.

Director: And then we see how they react?

Youth: That's right. If they accept the truth about this thing, then we can carry on toward other, bigger things.

Director: And if they won't accept this little truth?

Youth: Not even after several tries? We have to stop.

15

Director: Is giving up on them a sign that we are weak?

Youth: It's not about how strong we are. It's all about not wasting strength on those who are not willing to accept the truth.

Director: Do you believe it's possible they'll come around in time?

Youth: Well, if they do, they'll do it on their own. And then they'll live with truth. They'll keep it fresh within, and will not contradict the truth in word or deed.

Director: What happens if they contradict the truth?

Youth: I think they suffer for the sin.

Director: The sin against the truth? What punishment is there?

Youth: They lose the strength they gained by walking with the truth.

Director: Does that include their peace of mind?

Youth: They lose that, too.

Director: Is there a way to tell if they have lost their peace of mind?

Youth: They can't stand up to questioning. They get upset.

Director: You mean the ones who walk with truth are happy to respond to anything you ask?

Youth: Well, mostly anything. The others do not want their lies exposed. It's fear of this that robs them of their peace.

Director: I see. How often do you think that we'll succeed in helping people live the truth?

Youth: Not very often, I'm afraid.

Director: Is it more likely that we would succeed in helping people take a single step toward the truth?

Youth: That's much more likely, I would say.

Director: Now tell me this. For us to help would our path have to cross with theirs, or do we leave our path to meet them on their own?

Youth: We have to keep to our own path.

Director: And if we're walking with the truth, the paths would intersect at points of truth?

Youth: Of course.

Director: So there's some hope for those that we encounter on our way? I mean, they made it to a point of truth all on their own.

Youth: That's right.

Director: Suppose we're walking on our way, in truth, and suddenly a man who often walks with lies appears. Do we just out and out tell truth to him, or do we leave him well enough alone?

Youth: You mean he stops his lies and walks with truth at just this point? We do tell truth to him, if we are strong enough.

Director: What sort of strength would this require?

Youth: It takes a certain confidence in our own way. We cannot let the one we're speaking with divert us from our path if he sets out along the way of lies again. I think it's like when you attempt to save a drowning man. You cannot let him pull you down. He has to let you help.

Director: And how exactly do we save the drowning man?

Youth: We tell him truth, and nothing but the truth.

Director: And that's enough to buoy him?

Youth: I think it has to be.

Director: A lie will bring you down, while truth will lift you up?

Youth: Of course.

Director: But why would drowning men not always grab the truth?

Youth: Because they're panicking.

Director: Because they have no peace?

Youth: I think that's right.

Director: And they don't have the strength to swim, with all their heavy lies?

Youth: They don't.

Director: So they must calm themselves and drop the lies, then clutch the truth and float. But what if they attempt to hold the lies while clinging to the truth? Can lies bring down the truth that's meant to save their lives?

Youth: They can. The truth alone can't save a man. He has to help himself as well. So we can offer truth, but then it's up to him.

Director: And if the man is saved, what then?

Youth: He either will express his gratitude or run away.

Father: Or run away? But why?

Youth: Because he is ashamed he didn't have the truth.

Father: The only shame is acting like you are in ignorance once you have come to know the truth.

Director: Now let me ask you, Youth. This truth the man who's saved has come to know, does it involve the greater truths?

Youth: It does.

Father: But what exactly are the greater truths?

Director: The truths about the most important things.

Father: And what are they?

Director: Let's say for now they're anything that someone cherishes.

Father: And if somebody cherishes a lie?

Director: Then that is very difficult.

Father: He has to learn to cherish truth?

Director: Don't you agree?

Father: But what if truth seems not as sweet?

Director: Do you believe that lies are sweeter than the truth?

Youth: Of course they're not. The truth is what is sweet.

Director: But do you think it's sweet to everyone?

Youth: It ought to be.

Director: I wonder, now. Have you not heard about acquired tastes?

Youth: I have.

Director: Is sweetness an acquired taste?

Youth: I wouldn't say it is. Most people like sweet things from when they're very young.

Director: And what of bitter things?

Youth: You mean like bitter truths?

Director: I do. Is bitter always bad?

Youth: With truth I'd say it is.

Director: But still, do you believe it's possible for someone to get used to bitterness?

Youth: Who wants a bitter truth?

Father: Well, no one wants a bitter truth. But sometimes you must learn to live with one.

Director: Do you believe it's possible that over time the bitter truth turns sweet?

Father: You mean it isn't that you come to like the bitterness as bitterness, but rather that the flavor of the truth itself turns sweet?

Director: I do. What do you think?

Father: I'd like to think it's possible.

Director: But you don't think it is?

Father: It seems impossible, my friend.

Director: Well, maybe there's a change in how we taste, in time.

Father: What do you mean?

Director: I mean, suppose that truth is always sweet. But we must learn to taste it properly before it seems that way to us.

Father: All truth is sweet? That truly is impossible.

Director: So truth is sometimes bitter?

Father: Yes, of course.

Director: And bitterness is always bad?

Father: It's as we've said.

Director: Now here's a question, Youth. Do you believe it's possible to live your life so that you simply taste the truths we know are sweet? Or must you, of necessity, taste bitterness as well?

Youth: I don't know, strictly speaking, if it's necessary that you taste the bitter truths. But even if it is, I think we have to strive to taste as much of sweet as possible, with just the bare amount of bitterness.

Director: Is there a way to know ahead of time the way a thing will taste?

Youth: Well, we could smell the truth to get a sense.

Director: And if it smells so bad it makes you sick?

Youth: Then I would never taste that truth.

Director: Because you trust your sense of smell.

Youth: That's right.

Director: But you're aware not every bitter truth has got an evil smell?

Youth: I am.

Director: Suppose you taste a truth like that. Can you just spit it out and act as though you never tasted it?

Youth: No, you would have to learn from it. You'd have no choice.

Director: It's possible to learn from everything you taste?

Youth: It is. And I would even say it's possible to learn from everything you simply smell.

Director: Now, once we've learned, what do we do with truth?

Youth: I think we have to honor it.

Director: What does it take to honor truth?

Youth: I'd rather you tell me.

Director: I say you tell it when you can, and never contradict the truth, except . . .

Youth: Except?

Director: Except when you have reason to.

Youth: When you have reason to? What sort of reason could you have?

Director: At times it seems you have to contradict a lesser truth in order to reveal a greater truth.

Youth: I'd like a good example, please.

Director: If someone says it's cold, and someone else declares it's hot, can both be right, can both be speaking truth?

Youth: Of course.

Director: But they are contradicting one another, yes?

Youth: They are.

Director: What greater truth can come to sight because these two are so opposed?

Youth: The truth that different people often feel quite differently despite the fact that the environment's the same.

Director: Would it be good, if I am cold, to say it's hot because another says it's so, and he is speaking truth for him?

Youth: Of course that isn't good. You have to speak the truth you know. You have to speak it honestly.

Director: Now, do you think the point of this is that the truth is relative?

Youth: For certain things I think it is.

Director: And when the truth is relative there will be contradictions, no?

Youth: I think there will.

Director: Suppose that someone cherishes a truth that's relative, and then suppose you contradict this truth. Will there be trouble, Youth?

Youth: I think there will be, yes.

Director: Can it be helped, if you are speaking truth for you?

Youth: No, I don't think it can.

Director: But let's suppose you contradict yourself.

Youth: You mean I hold two views that are opposed? I'd have to clear this up.

Father: Not everything that is opposed can be cleared up, my boy. The truth is sometimes paradoxical.

Youth: So we must live this paradox?

Father: At times we must.

Youth: But what if you don't want to live a paradox?

Father: Well, you won't always have a choice.

Youth: But can't you use your mind to fight the paradox? The mind is rational. It uses logic to proceed. With logic you are not supposed to contradict yourself.

Father: You think that logic always leads to truth?

Youth: It often does.

Director: So when does logic fail?

Youth: When it has got a premise wrong.

Director: How do you check your premises?

Youth: Through reasoning, and gut.

Director: You have to use both eyes?

Youth: You do. Logicians often only see with just their mind.

Director: And for the other eye, did we not say a gut that's fed on reasoning is best?

Youth: We did. But that's the problem here. The reasoning must be correct.

Director: What happens when it's not?

Youth: The gut gets sick?

Director: And if logicians feel they have to choose between their mind and gut?

Youth: They choose the mind.

Director: But let's suppose there is no conflict here. Suppose the mind is strong in proper reasoning, and that the gut is fed on this.

Youth: A man who's got a mind and gut like that would be a champion of truth.

Director: Assuming he is not an evil man?

Youth: Of course.

Director: Because the evil can use logic, proper logic, too? Or do they always have a premise wrong?

Youth: I'd like to think they always have a premise wrong.

Director: What premise would this be?

Youth: I couldn't say.

Director: Perhaps it will occur to us as we proceed. Now, you agree that evil men can have strong guts?

Youth: I do, and they are evil guts.

Director: Then what are we to do when faced with logic from an evil man who's very powerful in mind and gut?

Youth: We run.

Director: But short of that?

Youth: If we're not strong enough to take him on in argument, we simply state the truth, devoid of reasonings to lend support.

Director: The simple truth shall set us free?

Youth: It shall, or so I like to think when it's our only hope.

16

Director: Is truth so bad a hope?

Youth: Well, you can bury truth in lies.

Director: Does it take many lies to bury just a single truth?

Youth: I think it only takes a single lie. But then so many people pile on.

Director: You mean they all repeat the same old lie?

Youth: They do.

Director: And when a lie is told enough, it seems like truth?

Youth: It does.

Director: What does it take to make a lie like that appear to be a lie?

Youth: I think it takes an audience that's predisposed to truth, that's predisposed to give the truth a chance.

Director: And if this audience rejects the truth?

Youth: Then they are weak.

Director: You wouldn't say that it's the truth that's weak?

Youth: Of course I wouldn't, no. It's people who are weak, not truth.

Director: And people who are strong, do they accept the truth?

Youth: They do, when they are strong in all that matters most.

Director: Now what about the vast majority? Is it not strong?

Youth: I wouldn't say that it accepts the truth.

Director: Why not?

Youth: It's by and large composed of people who are not that strong alone.

Director: But as a larger entity, a group, is it not open to the truth?

Youth: It thinks it knows the truth, and that there is no truth except for what it knows.

Director: But doesn't it in fact know many truths?

Youth: It does. But there are truths it overlooks.

Director: What are these truths?

Youth: I can't explain them very well.

Director: That's fine. But does the vast majority just overlook these truths, or is it truly blind to them?

Youth: It's truly blind.

Director: And does this blindness of the vast majority cause harm?

Youth: It does.

Director: Has it caused harm to you?

Youth: It has. The vast majority can't see me as I truly am.

Director: And that's the harm? Perhaps you ought to take revenge for that.

Youth: Revenge? Against the vast majority? But how?

Director: When is it necessary to be seen for what you are?

Youth: It's always necessary, right?

Director: However that may be, let's think of an example here. Does nothing come to mind?

Youth: Not right away.

Director: Well, I have one. Let's say it's when you want a custom suit.

Youth: A custom suit?

Director: Why, sure. The suit must fit. In order for the suit to fit the tailor has to see you for exactly what you are.

Youth: The tailor is the vast majority?

Director: He is. And he's the only tailor to be found.

Youth: Then I am out of luck. The suit will never fit.

Director: I think you're giving up a bit too easily, my friend.

Father: The answer's simple, Youth. You have to make your own.

Youth: But I don't know the way to make a suit.

Father: You'll have to learn.

Director: What would it take? Let's break it down.

Youth: Well, first I'd have to take my measurements.

Director: And then?

Youth: And then I'd have to learn to sew.

Director: What else?

Youth: I guess I'd need a pattern, right?

Director: It seems that's best. So how are we to sum it up? The measurements are truth?

Youth: They are.

Director: And sewing is an art?

Youth: It is.

Director: The pattern, can we say it is your plan?

Youth: Of course.

Director: And so to have a suit all of your own, a suit that fits you well, you need to have the truth, an art, and something of a plan.

Youth: Agreed.

Director: Now how do you believe the tailor will react when he learns what you've done?

Youth: I don't think that he'll like it very much.

Director: And every time he hears another praising your new suit?

Youth: It's going to rub him wrong.

Director: Is this revenge enough for you?

Youth: Assuming I can really make a proper suit? It is. And it is sweet.

Director: Is there another way to find a suit?

Youth: Well, I could always buy one off the rack.

Director: But that won't fit as well?

Youth: It won't.

Director: And why is that?

Youth: Because it wasn't made specifically for me.

Director: Would you call such a suit conventional?

Youth: I would, in both the fit and likely in the style.

Director: What is convention, Youth?

Youth: It's the agreed upon.

Director: The truth, is it conventional?

Youth: Of course it isn't, no.

Father: But can't we be agreed on truth?

Youth: Well, when we are that's not convention, right? It's simply truth.

Director: And when it isn't simply truth what do we do? Do we just go along?

Youth: Of course we don't. We must resist.

Director: And we do this alone?

Youth: We often do. But then we find the ones who live upon convention's border lines and win them over to the cause.

Director: The cause? What cause is that?

Youth: The cause of truth.

Director: What do we tell the borderline conventional to win them over thus?

Youth: We simply tell the truth, and they are won.

Director: Because they long for truth?

Youth: They do.

Director: Why can't they find it on their own?

Youth: I couldn't say. They simply can't.

Director: But if they can't, how do they know we're telling truth and not another lie?

Youth: They know because it resonates with them.

Director: And lies can never resonate?

Youth: Well, I'm not sure. Some lies are very plausible. They seem like truth.

Director: But let's suppose we speak the truth to them and they accept this truth as true. Could they be shocked at what they learn?

Youth: I think they could be, yes.

Director: So maybe it is best to feed the truth to them a little at a time?

Youth: Oh, I agree. I think it takes some time for them to take it in.

Director: And once they're used to truth they join with us and fight the false?

Youth: I think they must.

Director: Or else?

Youth: Or else they are not servants of the truth.

Director: What makes them want to serve the truth?

Youth: It gives them strength.

Director: They feel this right away when they begin to serve?

Youth: I think they do.

Director: Then wouldn't everybody seek to serve the truth if they're aware that it will give them strength?

Youth: Not everyone's aware. What more, not everyone can live up to the truth.

Director: It takes a certain strength to gain this sort of strength?

Youth: It does.

Director: It takes a little seed?

Youth: That's right.

Director: And those who merely are conventional in things that really count don't have this seed?

Youth: They don't. Conventions are not true.

Director: They're never true?

Youth: Conventionality is like a lie that's mingled with some truth. It's plausible. But it's not really true.

Director: You'd take a stand against conventionality in every form?

Youth: I like to think I would, when it concerns important things.

Director: You hope that truth will one day be the norm for these important things?

Youth: Don't you?

Director: I hope that truth will one day come to those who're strong enough to handle it and thrive.

Youth: What happens if it comes to those who're weak?

Director: The pearls are cast among the swine.

Youth: What if the truth comes late to those who're strong?

Director: Are you afraid it might come late to you?

Youth: I am.

Director: It's better late than never, right?

Youth: But then I might not have the time I need to reach my excellence.

Director: Your excellence? Do you believe that you have excellence within, an excellence that needs the truth to come into its own?

Youth: I like to think I do.

Director: This excellence of yours, whatever it might be, suppose it's only recognized once you are gone.

Youth: You mean when I am dead?

Director: Exactly so. Would you be satisfied?

Youth: I guess — except I'd never know I won.

Director: You won? The battle to achieve your excellence? Or do you mean the battle to be recognized?

Youth: Well, both.

Director: You first must reach your excellence and only then can you be recognized?

Youth: Of course.

Director: And so it's best to focus on the excellence. And once you're very sure of that, you'll try to get the other thing. But there's a science to these things, you know.

Youth: Please tell me more.

Director: An excellence derives from truth. And truth has got a power all its own. Do you agree?

Youth: I do.

Director: And truth can be a seed?

Youth: Of course.

Director: So if you place your truth in fertile soil, the odds are that it grows?

Youth: That's true. What happens then?

Director: The truth grows up and spreads its seeds. Then from these seeds more truths might grow. And so on and again.

Youth: And all this truth supports your excellence, and makes it possible that you'll be recognized?

Director: Don't you agree?

Youth: This science of the truth, it's really agricultural?

Director: That's how it seems to me.

Youth: Then what about the sun and rain the seeds require for their growth?

Director: I'll tell you now. But I don't think you'll like what I have got to say.

They both are simply luck.

Youth: What science is dependent on mere luck?

Director: The noblest kind.

Youth: So we must spread the seeds of truth both far and wide, for luck to have a chance?

Director: That's how it seems.

Youth: But then we simply play the odds — so many seeds, so many shoots across a broad expanse?

Director: And what is wrong with that?

Youth: I guess there's nothing wrong with that. So if I spread my seeds of truth I know that some will grow and spread their truth in turn, and victory is guaranteed?

Director: There is no guarantee.

Youth: Is there another way?

Director: There is. It might be best to focus on a little patch of ground, and lavish all your care on just the small amount of seeds that fit the plot. But either way, it's not a given that the truth will grow. Or do you think it is?

Youth: No, I don't think it is.

Director: Since that's the case, what greater reason do you need to strive concerning truth?

Youth: Why, none.

Director: And when it's time to die what do you have?

Youth: You have some hope that what you've sown will grow?

Director: Is that so bad?

Youth: No, not so bad.

Director: Now tell me, Youth. Must you have doubt in order to have hope?

Youth: I never thought of it like that, but yes. If you have got no doubt, if you have certainty, then you have got no need for hope.

Director: We hope when we don't know.

Youth: We do. But sometimes we despair.

Director: What reason is there for despair?

Youth: There's never reason for despair.

Director: So one should always hope?

Youth: I think that's true.

Director: What is the basis for this hope?

Youth: The fact that it just takes a little seed.

Director: A seed of truth?

Youth: That's right. You have to nurture it. You have to lavish all your care on it.

Director: And what of all your truths that are mature? Why, do you have to lavish care on them as well?

Youth: No, I don't think you do. The sun and rain take care of them. So it's the seedlings you must watch.

Director: And that is even so if you have got a forest of tall trees?

Youth: It is. It's always best to nurture seeds of truth, regardless of how certain you might be with all of your tall trees.

Director: Because a life that has no hope is terrible?

Youth: That's so.

Director: That's even so if one is happy and quite healthy, too?

Youth: You can't be either of those things unless you have some hope.

Director: So hope's an element of health and happiness?

Youth: It is.

Director: Then we must always nurture hope.

17

Youth: The ones who nurture hope are strong.

Director: Aren't those who truly nurture anything at all quite strong?

Youth: I think they are. To nurture you have got to have a gentle touch. And everybody knows that gentleness requires strength.

Director: What if you nurture doubt?

Youth: Among opinions that are false? I think that's fine.

Director: What does it take to nurture doubt?

Youth: It's just another seed you sow.

Director: How do you sow this seed?

Youth: You point out problems in the view that someone holds.

Director: And that's enough?

Youth: It might be, yes.

Director: When we sow seeds of doubt what do we hope?

Youth: We hope to make the ones in question think.

Director: Can everybody think, or just a lucky few?

Youth: No, I believe that nearly everyone can think.

Director: So nearly everyone can know the truth?

Youth: The truth as it relates to them, they can.

Director: But is there truth beyond the relative?

Youth: There is.

Director: How do you come to know this truth?

Youth: You have to strive for it.

Director: Not everybody strives?

Youth: That's right.

Director: And if you reach this truth, what then?

Youth: You mean you simply reach the truth, the total truth? You're whole.

Director: Is love a part of total truth? I ask because it's often said that love will make you whole.

Youth: Of course it is. But love takes truth, and truth takes love.

Director: I see. And all of us, we all desire to be whole?

Youth: I'm not so sure. I mean, we don't all strive.

Director: Do you believe it's possible to teach another how to strive?

Youth: At most we simply sow some seeds of truth or doubt, and hope that that's enough encouragement.

Father: And what about the opposite? Suppose you are discouraged, Youth. Suppose you are a member of a group, a group that seeks to limit how you strive for truth. What do you do?

Youth: You either leave the group, or if you cannot leave, you break with it inside while outwardly remaining part.

Director: Do you believe we're always free to strive inside?

Youth: In theory, yes. But there are times when we're so terrorized outside we're not.

Director: The terror is when groups make clear that striving for the truth is not allowed, and then they punish quite severely those who try?

Youth: It is.

Director: And what's the opposite of this?

Youth: The opposite is when a group supports you in your quest for truth.

Director: Then what's the middle ground?

Youth: The group just leaves you well enough alone.

Director: And that's not bad.

Youth: No, that's not bad.

Director: Now, what about the number of the strivers in a given group? Does that much matter, Youth?

Youth: I think it does.

Director: If there are more the group will likely be supportive of your quest?

Youth: It will.

Director: If there are less then persecution is more likely to ensue?

Youth: That's right. And then the worst is when there are no strivers in the group at all.

Director: Now what about the strength of all these groups? Do you believe the group itself is stronger when it has a lot of those who strive?

Youth: If they can act together, yes.

Director: What would that take?

Youth: A common vision of the truth.

Director: And this would make them strong?

Youth: Of course.

Director: But strong enough to stand up to aggressive challenges from other groups?

Youth: Well, they'd need other strengths, as well.

Director: And if our group is dedicated to the truth, would it in turn attack the false in all these other groups? Or would it leave them well enough alone?

Youth: I think that it would fight the false.

Director: And what if all these other groups agree and thus create a truth?

Youth: Create a truth? I don't know what you mean.

Director: Why, through the act of valuing. Have you not heard that value that's agreed upon, for instance in the marketplace, is truth?

Youth: But those who strive are not concerned with truths like that.

Director: They don't care what an apple costs?

Youth: Well, sure they do. But that is not their main concern.

Director: Their main concern, for instance, is the truth that money can't buy love?

Youth: That is the sort of truth they care about.

Director: They care about the priceless truth, the truth beyond the relative?

Youth: They do.

Father: But they must live. And life exacts a price.

Youth: They're well aware of that.

Director: What will they do?

Youth: They must find jobs.

Director: What sort of jobs?

Youth: Why, any sort that suits them well.

Director: What sort of job suits you?

Youth: The kind that only takes my mind. A job like yours.

Director: You think it only takes my mind?

Youth: It takes your body, too?

Director: Of course it does. It takes a fair amount of stamina.

Youth: But what takes stamina? I mean, you just direct at work, correct?

Director: I do direct. But I have got to deal with people, Youth. And that takes strength.

Youth: Because the people all oppose how you direct?

Director: Not all of them. A handful do. Though some of them are relatively powerful within the company.

Youth: But they're not powerful in truth?

Director: You have a point. They're often not.

Youth: How do you deal with them?

Director: I speak the truth.

Youth: And do they take that as a bold attack?

Director: They sometimes do.

Youth: What happens then?

Director: There's trouble then.

Youth: What else can happen when you speak the truth to those not strong in truth?

Director: Good things can sometimes come of it.

Youth: What does it take for that?

Director: The one I'm speaking to must have some doubts about the things he doesn't know.

Youth: You mean he can't believe he knows the things he doesn't know.

Director: That's right.

Youth: And so the strength of truth for good is based on doubt?

Director: It seems it is, when doubt's a starting point.

Youth: But do you always come to know through doubt? What if you're starting from the truth?

Father: How would you know that it's the truth if you don't ever doubt that truth?

Youth: So we must have our doubts if we would have the truth.

Director: Can you see any other way?

Youth: I can't.

Director: Now, those who've never had a doubt are what?

Youth: I think they are inhuman things. They are impervious to truth. They might as well be made of stone.

Director: How many do you think are made of stone, are petrified?

Youth: Completely petrified? I guess that's somewhat rare. But there are many who are partly so.

Director: Is there a way from stone to flesh and blood?

Youth: No, if you've never had a doubt, that part of you, once stone, cannot be brought to life.

Father: But I believe it's possible for it to come to life.

Director: What happens if it does?

Father: The person will need comforting.

Director: And why is that?

Father: It can be terrible to go from certainty to doubt. It's likely that you'll suffer from a sort of vertigo.

Director: And what of all your time without a doubt?

Father: It seems to be a waste. But you can salvage something from your stony past.

Youth: Like what?

Father: A seed of truth. A seed that gives you hope.

Youth: You mean that it just sat upon the stone for all that time and did not die?

Father: I like to think that's possible.

Director: This seed is all you take with you from your old life of certainty?

Father: It is. With this you start afresh. You must use all your strength and care to make it grow.

Director: But as your truth is growing, will you doubt this truth?

Youth: I think you will. But you will see it with your very eyes and come to knowledge of your truth, eventually. We all must use our eyes to see and come to know our truths.

Director: Do you believe you see your truth?

Youth: I have my doubts.

Director: Should we explore these doubts?

Youth: Perhaps some other time?

Director: That's fine. Should we explore a doubt that I have got?

Youth: We should. What is this doubt?

Director: It is the doubt that's born of solitude.

Youth: Can you say more?

Director: I doubt when I am all alone in what I think is true.

Youth: What do you do about your doubt?

Director: I check with everyone I know.

Youth: But what if what you think is controversial?

Director: You believe I shouldn't try to find the truth if what I think is controversial?

Youth: No. You ought to try. But don't you have to hide the full extent of what you think and simply check your premises?

Director: You mean I just don't draw conclusions when I talk about my doubts?

Youth: I do.

Director: I only tell a partial truth?

Youth: I think you're forced to carry on this way.

Director: Because the truth I doubt might cause me trouble were it known? But don't you think that is a sort of lie?

Youth: Well, if it is it is a noble lie.

Director: Because it spares me from the lovers of the false?

Youth: That's right.

Director: And once I've checked my premises, I draw conclusions on my own and share them with my friends?

Youth: That's how it ought to be.

Director: And are my friends and I a sect that revels in a hidden truth?

Youth: Why, no. We share it when we can, when it's not dangerous.

Director: And how are we to know when it's not dangerous?

Youth: We just reveal a little of the truth at first.

Director: And then a little more? And then a little more?

Youth: Don't you agree that's how it has to be?

Director: That seems to be the prudent way. But tell me, Youth. What makes it so we can proceed as we reveal the truth?

Youth: The people that we're talking to, when they agree with what we say.

Director: But what if they agree but do not understand? Or worse — what if they lie and say that they agree?

Youth: We have to have a way to know they understand.

Director: We have to have a way to know what's in their soul? Or isn't that where understanding lives?

Youth: No, I believe it is.

Director: The heart and mind are part of soul?

Youth: They are.

Director: Both heart and mind can understand?

Youth: Of course.

Director: What do we say of those who do not understand?

Youth: We say they're ignorant.

Director: They're ignorant in mind?

Youth: That's right.

Director: They're ignorant in heart?

Youth: That seems a little strange to say.

Director: But is it true?

Youth: I think it is.

Director: Now what is stronger, Youth, the hearts and minds that understand or those that don't?

Youth: The ones that understand, of course.

Director: But can't the ignorant be strong in their own way?

Youth: But how?

Director: Why, through their stubbornness, like mules.

Youth: So strength is not enough?

Director: It seems it's not. What else is needed here?

Father: A heart and mind receptive to the truth.

18

Director: What makes a heart or mind receptive, Youth?

Youth: Your nature, and the choices that you make.

Director: Well, nature can't be helped. But we can try to influence the choices that a person makes.

Youth: We can. We have to speak persuasively.

Director: We do indeed.

Father: We can't forget that nurture plays a role.

Director: Of course. How do we nurture someone toward the truth?

Youth: We teach him that it's valuable.

Director: By valuing the truth ourselves?

Youth: That's right. We model the behavior that we teach.

Director: Suppose our pupil doesn't follow us.

Youth: I guess that means his nature isn't good.

Director: And we're the judge of that?

Youth: Who else?

Director: What do we do if we're agreed his nature is no good?

Youth: We find a pupil with a better nature, then.

Director: Because we can't afford to waste our time?

Youth: That's right. There's only time enough to nurture natures that are good.

Director: What happens to the natures that are bad?

Youth: They soon become the mules that you were speaking of — or worse.

Director: There's no preventing that, not even with a patient nurturing?

Youth: A mule's a mule.

Director: So nature is the thing.

Youth: It is.

Director: What happens when a nature that is good receives no proper nurturing?

Father: Its soul is unrefined.

Director: You mean it's coarse?

Father: I do.

Director: Does it much matter if it's coarse, as long as it aligns with truth?

Youth: No, truth's the thing.

Father: But can this soul align with subtle truths?

Director: The truth itself is subtle, friend? Or is it in the way that you employ the truth that subtlety is found?

Youth: I think it's in the way that you employ the truth.

Director: Now, why not just be bold in truth?

Father: A subtle touch at times is more appropriate.

Director: And only souls that are refined can have a subtle touch?

Father: That's right.

Director: And only souls that are refined can understand, appreciate, a subtle touch?

Father: I'm not so sure.

Director: Do you believe that many are refined?

Father: Not many, no.

Director: Is that because there aren't that many natures that are good? Or is the nurturing the rarer thing?

Father: It is the combination of the two that's rare.

Director: Now, if a lucky man has got them both, can he do things that others can't?

Father: He can.

Director: You'd say that he has special skills?

Father: I would.

Director: And are these useful skills or useless skills?

Father: They're useful skills, of course.

Director: These useful skills, are they of use because they help him do what he would like to do? Or are they useful in some other way?

Father: They help him do what he would like to do.

Director: And doing what he'd like to do means being what he'd like to be? Or are we different than the things we do?

Father: No, we are what we do.

Director: Does it take will, or drive, to be whatever you would be?

Father: It does.

Director: So if you have a nature and a nurture that is good, and you have got the drive, it's possible to be whatever you would like to be?

Youth: What if you want to be the president?

Father: Well, that would take a great amount of will.

Director: Perhaps we ought to say again just what we mean by strength of will.

Youth: The fact that you will not let go. You are tenacious like a bulldog.

Director: That's a virtue, right?

Youth: Depending on what you have sunk your teeth into.

Director: And if you sink your teeth into the truth?

Youth: You look to the example of the dog.

Director: The dog, indeed. But now I fear we've done injustice to the mule.

Youth: How so?

Director: We criticized the mule for stubbornness in ignorance. But what if he won't budge because he knows he's standing on the truth?

Youth: Then there are times that we should be like mules.

Director: So then, just focus on the truth, hang on with all your might, and see how things turn out?

Youth: That's not the way it goes for those who would be president.

Director: You mean they don't hang on to truth?

Youth: To put it mildly, yes.

Father: But what if someone held on tight to truth and it turned out, by some great strokes of luck, that he became the president?

Youth: I think that it takes more than that.

Director: What does it take?

Youth: He needs some of the baser strengths.

Director: The baser strengths?

Youth: The physical, as far as great endurance goes, and money backing him.

Director: I think you're right. He needs these things. What else?

Father: He needs the art of winning friends — a million friends and more.

Youth: But how can someone have so many friends? That's just a lie. The friendships are not true.

Father: You think that presidents must always live a lie?

Youth: Don't you?

Father: I'm not so sure. It seems to me a president might truly be the friend of many, many men.

Youth: What do they have in common, then?

Father: Why, don't you know? Their characters. Or don't you think that that's enough to base a friendship on?

Youth: Of course I do. But I don't know.

Director: What don't you know?

Youth: We're saying that the characters of all these friends are good?

Father: We are.

Youth: Good character's in short supply.

Director: Perhaps we'll say our voters of good character, while not in the majority, can swing a vote that's close.

Youth: I think that's more the thing.

Director: Now tell me, Youth. Are you that different than a president who holds himself to truth?

Youth: You mean he really lives the truth, and not just "truth?" I guess I'm not, essentially. I hold on tight to truth — at least I try.

Director: But do you think you want to be the president?

Youth: I don't.

Director: Why not?

Youth: Why not? Don't make me laugh!

Director: Is living truth tenaciously success enough for you?

Youth: I like to think it is.

Father: But it takes more than that to be successful in this life.

Director: What does it take?

Father: For one, you need good health — beyond mere stamina. It takes much more than truth to keep your mind and body sound.

Director: Is health as basic of a thing as we can find?

Father: I think it is. It is the bedrock of our lives.

Director: And as the bedrock, when we build on it, we reach the higher things?

Father: We do.

Director: Is love a higher thing?

Father: Well, love's a funny thing. Without my health, I still would love my son.

Director: So love is much more basic than your health?

Father: It is.

Director: But must you be quite strong to love?

Father: You must.

Director: But if you've lost your health, where do you get your strength?

Youth: You'll always have your moral strength.

Director: Is moral strength like strength of will?

Youth: It is, but not exactly so. Your will can be attached to something bad.

Director: But love is always good?

Youth: When you feel love you know it's good, no matter what.

Director: And why is that?

Youth: It's just the way it works.

Director: What if you fall in love with someone who's a criminal?

Youth: Then there would have to be a part of her that isn't criminal, a part that's true — a part I love.

Director: So love is like a compass, Youth? It always points to truth?

Youth: That's what I think.

Director: But what if it is just a speck of truth amidst a larger lie? Or do you think a speck is not enough to pull you in?

Youth: A speck is not enough. For love, the truth is always more than that.

Director: And do you love just anyone with more than that?

Youth: I love the truth. Don't get me wrong. But I will only fall in love with what is mine.

Director: Your proper truth.

Youth: That's right.

Director: But what's this proper truth?

Youth: It's truth that's mine and only mine to know.

Director: Must you be strong to recognize this truth?

Youth: You must be very strong. Not everybody sees his proper truth.

Director: What sort of strength does it require?

Youth: A total being strength.

Director: You heart, and soul, and mind, and gut? Your everything?

Youth: Your everything.

Director: And that is love, your everything?

Youth: Of course.

Director: And what you love in someone else is truth?

Youth: It is.

Director: Suppose you met a woman with a body that is very beautiful. Is that the sort of truth that you could love?

Youth: Unless she has the other qualities I seek, then no.

Director: What other qualities?

Youth: A character that's good. A heart and mind attuned to truth. The things that we've been speaking of.

Director: Suppose that she has eyes that flash with bold intelligence. Would that not draw you in despite the fact she lacks the other things you say you want?

Youth: I want the things I want.

Director: You are devoted to your truth.

Youth: I am.

Director: I think that's very good. I hope it brings you happiness.

Youth: You hope? You mean that you don't think devotion is enough?

Director: In life the certainties are few.

Youth: But what about the truth?

Director: The truth may be you lose your health and love to accidents. Or do you think I've got it wrong?

Youth: No, I'm aware that what you say is possible. But if I lose those things, what have I got?

Director: You've got your mind, your character, your heart. You've got the things that we've been speaking of.

Father: Unless . . .

Youth: Unless?

Father: Unless you lose those things, as well.

Youth: But if you lose those things, it means you're weak.

Father: Some of the strongest break in time. Remember what we said about a man who lives in misery?

Youth: I do. Do you remember that I said you can be good and miserable at once?

Director: Of course we do. But why don't we explore the positive? From those who suffer from misfortune, is there something to be gained?

Youth: Like what?

Director: Perhaps they'll tell you things that others can't, or won't.

Youth: Because they have unique perspectives on the world?

Director: Don't you believe that's true?

Youth: I do. I've suffered some, you know.

Director: I do believe you have. So share your view. You might enlighten someone else.

Father: But really now, Director, it is as you've said — so many suffer in this world.

Director: But it is also true we bear our suffering quite differently.

Youth: How so?

Director: Why, there are those who'd never place their burden on another soul. They'd die before they'd do a thing like that. They take it up all by themselves. Don't you agree?

Father: Of course. And there are those who'd share their burden with a friend.

19

Youth: You think it's best to share your burden, Dad?

Father: I do.

Youth: But why?

Father: Besides the good that it would do for you? Your sharing makes your friend a stronger man.

Youth: But stronger how?

Father: He'll gain in spirit, Youth. He will be proud to help.

Director: And pride will make it pleasant to assist his friend?

Father: It will, most certainly.

Director: So friends give opportunity for pleasure when they share their suffering?

Father: That sounds a little odd, but I believe it's true.

Director: What happens if there only is a seed of friendship in the two?

Father: The sharing of the burden just might make it sprout.

Youth: But would you really take that risk? I'd want to know the man's a friend for sure before I'd share.

Director: How can you know if someone is your friend?

Youth: The values that he holds.

Director: Give me a good example of a value that you hold.

Youth: I try to listen to my conscience when it speaks.

Director: You try, or do you listen every time?

Youth: I try to listen every time — and I regret it when I don't.

Director: And when you're listening, what does your conscience say?

Youth: It tells me what to do.

Director: And you would have a friend whose conscience tells him what to do, as well?

Youth: I would. And I would have his conscience just as sensitive as mine.

Director: That all seems fine. I wonder, though. Does conscience tell you what to do, or not to do?

Youth: It tells me what I shouldn't do.

Director: So if your conscience says you shouldn't share your burden with a certain character, you wouldn't share your burden, right?

Youth: I guess.

Director: And if your conscience doesn't intervene, you're free to share?

Youth: But this sounds weird.

Director: What makes it weird?

Youth: You really think that it might harm my friend to share with him?

Director: The harm I'm thinking of is not so much to him.

Youth: The harm's to me? But conscience isn't for yourself. It's meant to stop your doing harm to others, right?

Director: It's meant to stop your doing harm to anyone at all — yourself especially.

Youth: I've never heard it put that way.

Director: Well, now you have. The question, though, is do you think it's true?

Father: I think it's true. And I'd go further, too. I'd say that conscience isn't simply negative.

Director: You mean that conscience positively tells you what to do?

Father: I do.

Youth: But how does it do that?

Father: Do you regret the things you do but shouldn't do?

Youth: Of course.

Father: And what about the things you ought to do but don't? Do you regret them, too?

Youth: I do.

Father: Regret's the same in either case?

Youth: Regret's regret.

Father: And conscience tries to keep you from regret?

Youth: I take your point. Your conscience tells you what to do.

Director: But does that mean that if there's nothing on your conscience then you're lost?

Youth: Well, I don't know.

Director: What makes it so that we're not lost?

Youth: Our hearts and minds — our compass and our chart.

Director: But if the conscience speaks it overrules our hearts and minds?

Youth: I wouldn't put it that way, no.

Director: The three must work together, then?

Youth: They must.

Director: So what about our burden, Youth? With conscience it is obvious — we say that something weighs on it, correct?

Youth: Correct.

Director: Now what about with heart and mind? Can something weigh on them, as well?

Youth: Of course. It's possible to have a heavy heart, to have some things that weigh upon your mind.

Director: And so, at best, your heart and mind and conscience are all free of weights, of worries, and all care?

Youth: Well, you should always take good care.

Director: Of course. But not excessive care?

Youth: Agreed.

Director: So how does all of this relate to strength?

Youth: What do you mean?

Director: Suppose you have a heart that's very strong. If there are things that weigh on it, can it be light despite the weight?

Youth: A stronger heart can bear a greater load more easily.

Director: And this is so with mind, as well?

Youth: It is.

Director: But what about the conscience?

Youth: Strength is not a factor here.

Director: But why?

Youth: Because it's sensitivity that counts.

Director: A conscience that is sensitive can bear a greater load?

Youth: Oh no, a conscience that is sensitive can only bear the lightest sort of load.

Director: Insensitivity is strength?

Youth: I don't like how that sounds.

Director: But is it true?

Youth: I don't believe it is. You cannot claim to bear a thing that you can't even feel.

Director: You only bear the things you feel?

Youth: Just so.

Director: Then why don't we all learn to numb ourselves?

Youth: It doesn't work like that. If you have got capacity to feel, no matter how you numb yourself, the burden mounts.

Director: And we don't want a burden on our consciences.

Youth: We don't.

Director: It's very odd. The more that we can feel, the more that we might bear. But then again, the more that we can feel, the less that we can bear, because we're very sensitive and can't stand much upon our consciences. And if you cannot feel, you cannot bear. So no one bears a great amount upon his conscience, then?

Youth: The point is that we all should have a conscience that is clear.

Director: Except we feel that evil men should bear great weight upon their consciences?

Youth: They ought to suffer from the weight.

Director: But if they simply don't have consciences? Can we impose a conscience on an evil man?

Youth: I don't see how that's possible.

Director: Can we impose a conscience on a man who's good?

Youth: I don't think consciences can be imposed.

Director: They grow up naturally?

Youth: I guess.

Director: But nurture helps?

Youth: Of course. But certain people can't be helped.

Director: The ones whose natures are quite bad?

Youth: That's right.

Director: So tell me this. Does conscience always lead to suffering?

Youth: Not if it's clear.

Director: Is conscience often clear?

Youth: Completely clear? I think that is exceptional.

Director: But if you haven't got a conscience then you're in the clear?

Youth: I think you're in for other suffering.

Director: Like what?

Youth: You'll get what you deserve.

Director: You mean that you'll do wicked things you wouldn't do if conscience had a say? And if you do these things you'll pay the price?

Youth: You will — or so I like to think.

Director: The universe exacts its toll, a sort of justice, no?

Youth: Again, I like to think it does.

Director: Has it exacted this on you?

Youth: Well, no.

Director: But have you seen this justice done to other men?

Youth: I haven't, no.

Director: Do you believe that many live without a conscience?

Youth: No. But I believe that many do not have a conscience that's as strict as mine.

Director: And so what's wrong for you is right for them?

Youth: No, wrong is wrong.

Director: They simply do not know it's wrong?

Youth: I'm not so sure.

Director: So how does conscience know when something's wrong?

Youth: I'd say it's something that is learned.

Director: From whom, your fellow men?

Youth: I think you learn it from yourself, and from the nature that you have, and from the nurture you receive.

Director: Do you learn this, The Golden Rule? Do unto others as you'd have them do to you?

Youth: That's very basic, yes.

Director: And if you do like that, you're strong in conscience, Youth?

Youth: I guess.

Director: But what if others don't reciprocate?

Youth: You keep on doing unto them and simply hope they come to do the same to you. But do you want to know the truth? I think that's wrong.

Director: What makes you say?

Youth: It shouldn't be a one-way street. If you don't get reciprocation over time, you need to stop.

Director: So if you have been more than fair to them, and they have not been fair to you, you grow unfair?

Youth: I think that's only fair, ironically.

Director: But how exactly would you be unfair? Would you not give them all what they deserve?

Youth: What they deserve? They don't deserve a single thing!

Director: So you would give to them what they deserve, which is precisely not a single thing.

Youth: I would.

Director: Then you would be quite fair to them.

Youth: I think you're right.

Director: But they believe that they deserve some good from us?

Youth: They do.

Director: Why do you think that is?

Youth: More often times than not? They think they're clever, and they think their cleverness deserves reward.

Director: Does cleverness deserve reward?

Youth: If it's associated with the truth, it does. But not when it's associated with a lie.

Director: I see. What makes a liar think that he is clever, Youth?

Youth: He thinks it's difficult to tell a lie and then maintain it, too. He also thinks it's difficult to know what lie to tell.

Director: Does it take brains to lie?

Youth: I don't think you have got to be especially intelligent.

Director: But if you want to lie and get away with it, you have to have some smarts?

Youth: I think you do. But someone who's intelligent can easily be caught. And someone who is rather dim can get away with it.

Director: So dim but smart, and bright but dumb?

Youth: That's often how it is.

Director: Which sort of man would you prefer to be your friend?

Youth: I don't think I would want a liar as my friend.

Director: Suppose that neither of them lies. Which one would you prefer? Intelligence or smarts?

Youth: I'd want the one with both.

Director: That's fair enough. How can you tell when someone is intelligent?

Youth: He understands a lot.

Director: A lot of what?

Youth: Of subjects that are difficult.

Director: Like math?

Youth: For instance, yes.

Director: And what about the difficulties in our lives, like death?

Youth: No, you don't have to be of great intelligence to come to terms with death.

Director: Aside from math, what else requires some intelligence?

Youth: The sciences.

Director: Can you be simply smart and grasp the sciences?

Youth: Not smart alone. You need intelligence.

Director: But not all scientists are smart.

Youth: Of course.

Director: What is intelligence?

Youth: Intelligence is just the power of the mind.

Director: The power of the mind? You mean it's like an engine, then?

Youth: Exactly so.

Director: So someone who's intelligent can figure out an abstract problem much more quickly than a man who's merely smart?

Youth: That's how I think it is.

Director: Well, what is smart?

Youth: It's when you know the way of things.

Director: The way of things? You mean a liar knows the way to lie to fool another man, and so he's smart?

Youth: I do.

Director: So smarts can be employed for good or ill.

Youth: They can, most certainly.

Director: And what about intelligence?

Youth: The same is true with it.

Director: Now tell me truly, Youth. If you could pick just one to be, which would it be?

Youth: I think that I'd pick smarts instead of raw intelligence.

Director: And why is that?

Youth: I'd rather know the way of things than win a race with other engines of the mind.

Director: Do you believe that all of the intelligent engage in races with each other, then?

Youth: I think they often do.

Director: And why is that?

Youth: They want to be the best, the most intelligent.

Director: The strongest in the mind?

Youth: That's right. But being smart is also strength.

Director: I'm sure it is.

20

Youth: Do you believe it's harder to be smart if you're intelligent?

Father: Intelligence can trip you up. You race through things and make assumptions all along the way.

Youth: At times it's best if you go slow?

Father: It is. Can you think when?

Youth: When you don't know the facts.

Father: That's right. You need to gather facts quite carefully. And even when you think you've got them all, there might be others you don't know about.

Youth: If that's the case, then when should you go fast?

Father: You want my honest answer, Youth?

Youth: Of course I do.

Father: I think it's best to take it slow in everything.

Youth: Then what's the use of having great intelligence, intelligence that makes you fast?

Director: It seems we're at a loss.

Youth: But you have great intelligence.

Director: Why, thank you for the compliment. And I think you are one of great intelligence.

Youth: Why thank you, too. But what's the use? I mean, if it is best to take things slow, then what am I to do with my intelligence?

Director: You mean you do not wish to make discoveries within the sciences?

Youth: But you have got to know the facts in order to achieve discoveries. And we are saying that you have to gather facts quite carefully, not quickly, right?

Father: But maybe when you've gathered up as many facts as possible, you let your mind go fast. You draw conclusions then.

Youth: But how are you to know you've gathered all of the important facts?

Father: You won't. That's why you must conclude provisionally, Youth.

Youth: So all of our intelligence just goes to make conclusions that we can't be sure about?

Director: Not all of our intelligence.

Youth: What else do we derive from our intelligence?

Director: A sense of humor.

Father: Humor is a useful thing. It's good to laugh.

Youth: That's all that our intelligence is for? To draw conclusions in the sciences and laugh?

Director: Is that not much?

Youth: But surely there is something more.

Director: Can you think what?

Youth: You're testing me. Well, what about a conversation like the one we're having now?

Director: Because we three are all of high intelligence? What comes of it?

Youth: We learn.

Director: But what exactly do we learn?

Youth: We learn . . . We learn . . .

Father: Perhaps we ought to learn to have a sense of humor, Youth.

Youth: Do you believe that I'm too serious?

Father: At times I think it wouldn't hurt to lighten up a bit.

Youth: But do you know the reason why I take things seriously?

Father: I don't.

Youth: Because I feel that my intelligence is my responsibility.

Director: You have to make the most of it?

Youth: I do.

Director: And how will you do that?

Youth: I wish I knew.

Director: Do other boys at school have high intelligence?

Youth: Of course.

Director: But they are not as serious as you?

Youth: They're not.

Director: And so you feel that you're alone?

Youth: I do.

Director: These other boys, do they go fast?

Youth: Of course they do.

Director: And do they stumble when they're going fast?

Youth: They don't believe they do — but, yes, they do.

Director: How can you tell?

Youth: I think about the things they say long after they've been said.

Director: And what do you discover when you do?

Youth: That what they've said makes little sense.

Director: I think we've found a better use for your intelligence.

Youth: Correcting what the others say?

Director: What's wrong with that?

Youth: They'll think that I'm a fool.

Director: But why?

Youth: Because when I approach them they'll have long forgotten all the things they've said.

Director: Then you'll remind them, right?

Youth: But then they'll ask why I don't speak up at the time.

Director: They'll ask why you aren't keeping up with them?

Youth: That is exactly what they'll ask.

Director: Will they make fun of you for being slow?

Youth: I think they will.

Director: Are you afraid of that?

Youth: I'm not.

Director: That's good. So is it settled then? You'll use your mind to check the carelessness of those who're fast?

Youth: Well, I'm not sure.

Director: Why not?

Youth: Is there no better use of my intelligence?

Father: This seems a noble use to me.

Youth: How so?

Father: You're bringing home the truth to those who rush. Is truth not noble, Youth?

Youth: Of course it is.

Father: And isn't it a noble thing to help another see the truth?

Youth: But that's the thing. These boys don't want the help.

Director: How can you tell?

Youth: They're satisfied with all the shortcuts that they take.

Director: Perhaps you'll make them feel dissatisfied.

Youth: I think they'll turn on me.

Director: Are you afraid of that?

Youth: I'm not — but it's not something I look forward to.

Director: But what if you can teach a number of these boys to slow things down? Is that not worth it, then?

Youth: I think it would be, yes. But I'm not sure that any of the faster boys will listen to a word I say.

Director: Well, what about the ones who cannot go as fast? Do you think there are some of them who're dedicated to the facts?

Youth: I do.

Father: Perhaps you'll laugh with them at those among the fast who turn on you.

Youth: We'll laugh at them for thinking that they know the truth?

Father: What else?

Youth: But if we laugh at them, they'll really start to hate us, no?

Director: You think it's better if you merely smile?

Youth: They'll think we're smug and hate us just as much.

Director: Do you think we can teach the fast to laugh with us at their mistakes?

Father: For that, they need to come to know the truth. There is no laughter without truth — no healthy laughter, anyway.

Director: Then it appears we have another use for our intelligence. We'll try to bring them to the truth and make them laugh.

Youth: But how can I do this if they've all turned on me?

Director: You'll have to tease them gently, Youth. Eventually your patience might pay off.

Youth: So this might be a waste of time?

Director: It's hard to say. But what if you enjoy the work? Is that a waste?

Youth: But you can't make another come to truth. All you can do is lay it out and hope he comes to see the truth for what it is. And then you have to hope he laughs.

Director: And if he laughs, what does it mean?

Father: It means he's confident enough to change his ways and bring himself in line with truth.

Youth: And if he doesn't laugh?

Father: He may be very serious about his fast and great intelligence and not be much inclined to change.

Youth: Then what are we to do with him?

Father: I think we have to keep on teasing him. Or do you think we just give up?

Youth: But what's our goal? To show him just how little his intelligence is worth?

Director: Why, no. We would encourage him to use his mind like us. Perhaps he can become a great supporter of the simple truth.

Youth: But what's the simple truth?

Director: It's that which comes from slow and careful thought.

Youth: Is there a time when slow and careful thought can make us first?

Father: Of course there is. There is a tie for first among the bravest souls who give themselves to truth this way.

Youth: What makes them brave?

Father: They stand their ground when they're confronted by the ones who turn on them.

Youth: The faster ones who lack a sense of humor, right?

Father: That's right.

Director: And what about the faster ones who have a sense of humor? Do they ever turn to us?

Father: Of course they do. They turn to us with jokes.

Youth: With inside jokes or jokes for all?

Father: With jokes for all — for all who get the jokes.

Director: Does it take strength to joke?

Father: A joke can be a very good reflection of your strength.

Youth: What sort of strength?

Father: The sort that gives you confidence enough to tell the joke.

Youth: But why do jokes require confidence?

Father: Because it's possible you'll be misunderstood.

Youth: It hurts when you're misunderstood.

Father: Not always, Youth. A healthy sense of irony can take away the pain.

Youth: So if you meant a thing to be a joke and someone takes it seriously and calls you on the quip, what can you do but laugh inside — ironically?

Father: Indeed.

Youth: But why won't you explain the joke?

Father: Because there is no point. The humor is already lost.

Director: But have you thought about the inverse situation, Youth?

Youth: What do you mean?

Director: Suppose that someone means a thing quite seriously, and yet it's taken as a joke. What then?

Youth: I'd say that that's ironic, too.

Director: Now, let me ask you this. When we tell lies can we be serious?

Youth: We can.

Director: And can we joke when we tell lies?

Youth: We can, but that seems strange.

Director: What makes it strange?

Youth: Why would you joke by telling lies?

Director: Comedians do this quite frequently. They tell amusing tales about the things they've done. In fact, they've never done these things.

Youth: That's true.

Director: Now let's forget about comedians. Let's say that you're the one who tells a lie, and that you tell it as a sort of joke. What truth can we expect from this?

Youth: There is no truth in this.

Father: Of course there is. The truth is in the laughter, Youth. Or don't you think that laughter, healthy laughter, has a truth that's all its own?

21

Youth: But then the truth comes at the cost of lies.

Director: I thought that you were of the view that we must purchase truth regardless of the cost.

Youth: I am. At least I think I am. I need to think about this more. But there is something more I want to say about intelligence.

Director: What's that?

Youth: Intelligence is not just speed. I mean, how can it be? We use intelligence when going slow.

Director: I think you have a point. So tell me what we gain when we take all the time we need concerning truth.

Youth: We gain in depth of comprehension, right?

Director: And who can make this gain?

Youth: Why, almost anyone — as long as he can think.

Director: Now, are there many things to comprehend in this, our world?

Youth: Of course there are.

Director: And does it do to comprehend just anything, or should we try to comprehend the most important things?

Youth: We ought to comprehend the most important things.

Director: What sort of things are most important, Youth?

Youth: The human things.

Director: You mean you have to comprehend your fellow man?

Youth: I do. But you must also comprehend yourself.

Director: Agreed. But can you ever fully comprehend another person's point of view?

Youth: I think you can, in broad strokes anyway.

Director: And this is so for everyone?

Youth: I think it's possible. We have a shared humanity.

Director: Remind us what it takes to comprehend.

Youth: Slow reasoning.

Director: How often do you think the fast slow down?

Youth: Not very frequently.

Director: And why is that? Do you believe that they don't want to comprehend?

Youth: They're bent on being fast, on being first. That's all they care about.

Director: Is there a way to make them want to comprehend their fellow men?

Youth: We might entice or tease them with the things that they don't know.

Director: And then they might suspect that comprehension's worth a whole lot more than being first?

Youth: A number of them will.

Director: A number that is great or small?

Youth: I think it's small.

Director: But it is better to win some of them than none?

Youth: Of course it is.

Director: Does it take strength to slow things down?

Youth: I think it does. You must apply the brakes with some amount of force.

Director: What happens when a man who's used to racing on ahead begins to comprehend the most important things?

Youth: I think that he's transformed.

Director: Well, so he is. Now, there is something that we haven't talked about along these lines, but should — our memory. Do we say memory is either strong or weak, or do we talk about it in another way?

Youth: We call it strong or weak.

Director: Is memory a part of your intelligence, or is it something else?

Youth: I think it's part of your intelligence.

Director: So if you're fast you have strong memory, and if you're slow your memory is weak? Is that the way it is?

Youth: I'm not so sure.

Director: Is that because a man who's slow in reasoning can have a memory that's strong?

Youth: It is. And those who're fast in reasoning quite often will forget the most important things.

Director: If you forget those things, what point is there in being fast, in being first?

Youth: There is no point.

Director: These things that we remember or forget, what are they, Youth?

Youth: The things we know.

Director: And we are strong when we remember what we know?

Youth: Of course.

Director: If we forget the things we know, do we still know, or are we ignorant again?

Youth: I think that we are ignorant, unless we can refresh our memory.

Director: And how do we refresh our memory?

Youth: We just remind ourselves of what we know.

Director: And that will keep us strong?

Youth: It will.

Director: Refreshing is an exercise for mind?

Youth: It is.

Director: Because the mind is like a muscle, yes?

Youth: I think it is. We have to keep it strong.

Director: Now, don't you think that all the knowledge in the world won't be of any use unless you can remember it, unless your memory is good?

Youth: I do.

Director: Do you believe there's more to strength of memory than just the exercise of it?

Youth: What do you mean?

Director: I mean, do you believe you have to organize the things you know? Or do you store the knowledge in your mind haphazardly?

Youth: I think you have to organize the things you know.

Director: Is there an art to organizing things?

Youth: I think there is.

Director: And what's the art?

Youth: You have to classify the things you know.

Director: What happens if you think at first a thing is X, but in the end you learn it's Y?

Youth: You mean you change the way you think of what you know? I guess you have reorganized your mind.

Director: And when you organize your mind, when is it strong? When what you know aligns with truth, or in some other way?

Youth: Your mind is strong when it aligns with truth.

Director: So if it's true that something is a Z, and in your mind, your memory, you know it as a Z, you're strong?

Youth: I think you have to be.

Director: Now tell me, Youth. Do many make the effort that it takes to organize their minds?

Youth: I think a number try, with varying success.

Director: What happens to the ones who do not even try?

Youth: Convention does the organizing, then.

Director: And if convention isn't always true?

Youth: Their minds won't be aligned with truth.

Director: Now here's the funny thing. The ones whose minds are not aligned with truth can often still remember many things.

Youth: That's true.

Director: So must we say their memories are strong?

Youth: But how can we say that?

Director: Why, in the same way that we say a bully can be strong. It's how you use your strength that counts. Don't you agree?

Youth: Of course. The strength of memory is just like any other strength. It can be used for good or ill. I mean, a liar stores up in his memory the many lies he tells so he can keep them straight.

Director: Now, can you guess what I'm about to ask?

Youth: You want to know if it is better for a man to have a memory that's strong for evil ends, or if it would be better for this man to have a memory that's relatively weak but dedicated to the good.

Director: Well, what's the answer, Youth?

Youth: It's better to be weak and serve the good.

Director: And how exactly do we serve the good?

Youth: By learning and remembering the truth.

Director: And if we happen to forget?

Youth: Then we must learn the truth again, but then refresh it all the time.

Director: Is there a way to live where you are constantly refreshing truth, so that you never can forget?

Youth: I think that is the secret art to life.

Director: How do we set to live this way?

Youth: For one, we choose our friends based on their love of truth.

Director: Then let me guess the rest. We simply must surround ourselves, as much as possible, with truth?

Youth: I think that's it. We always want the truth about the most important things to be refreshed. There is no better way to live.

Father: And what about the lesser things? I mean, I need to know the numbers to my combination lock.

Youth: Well, you can write them down.

Father: You can't write everything.

Youth: That's true. You simply have to do your best to memorize these things by rote.

Director: Now there are those who have a gift of memory for things like this. Don't you agree? It seems they just remember things, no special effort on their part.

Youth: Agreed. But it is often only for the less important things. It's like the ones who race ahead with their intelligence and miss the point. These gifted ones of memory are so caught up in all the little things they know that they don't focus on the most important things.

Father: They have to learn to use their gift, or else the gift becomes a curse. What use is memory if it distracts you from the greater truth?

Youth: No use that's any good. And I'll tell you another problem with strong memory. Suppose that you remember everything, both good and bad.

Father: The bad would be the curse? You mean you wish that you could just forget?

Youth: I do.

Father: You have to overcome the bad with good.

Youth: Suppose that there's a lot of bad.

Father: But don't you think that one strong memory of good outweighs a dozen of the bad?

Youth: But what if you have more than just a dozen of the bad?

Father: Well, I would say a memory of good that's very, very strong outweighs a thousand of the bad.

Director: The memory of good can be quite powerful.

Father: Indeed.

Director: But still, that doesn't mean you just forget the bad. Or does it, now?

Youth: Some things you simply can't forget.

Director: So what are we to do with our bad memories?

Youth: We have to learn from them?

Director: And if we learn from them will we be better at avoiding what is bad?

Youth: For certain things I think that's true.

Director: And if it is, can we then help our friends avoid the bad, as well?

Youth: In certain cases, yes.

Director: And what about the good?

Youth: Bad memories can help us to appreciate the good.

Director: And if we do appreciate the good, can we then help our friends to do the same?

Youth: We certainly can try.

22

Director: What makes it hard to learn from what another's learned?

Youth: You lack experience that brings the lesson home.

Director: You need to come to your own truth, not truth at second hand?

Youth: Exactly, yes.

Director: How do you feel when you arrive at your own truth?

Youth: You're satisfied.

Director: You're always satisfied?

Youth: I like to think you are.

Director: That's even when what brings you to your truth is bad?

Youth: You learn from what is bad, and learning in itself is always good.

Director: Suppose the truth you learn is less than flattering to you. Are you still satisfied?

Youth: I think you can be, yes, deep down inside, despite the fact the truth displeases superficially.

Director: But only if you're good deep down inside? I mean, will evil men appreciate the truth?

Youth: I know they won't.

Director: What makes the good appreciate the less than pleasant truth?

Youth: They simply value truth. They're willing to embrace the truth, to put themselves in line with truth. This is a core component of their character.

Director: In order to appreciate the truth you have to recognize the truth, correct?

Youth: Of course.

Director: What lets you recognize the truth?

Youth: Experience, both good and bad?

Director: Experience can teach the way that truths or lies will look, the way that they will feel?

Youth: I think that's true.

Director: Does it take long experience, or are there those who simply have a gift for recognizing truth from just the barest of experience?

Father: You mean they know the truth from when they're young?

Director: Don't you believe that's possible?

Father: For certain truths, perhaps.

Director: What do you think it's like for them, the ones who know?

Father: I think it can be lonely.

Director: How can they be sure they know the truth?

Father: They have to verify.

Director: Is this an easy thing when you are young?

Father: It isn't even easy when you're in the prime of life.

Director: What does it take?

Father: You simply have to prove the things you think you know — experiments and arguments.

Director: Suppose you think you know that someone isn't nice.

Youth: But can you really prove objectively that someone isn't nice? It's just a matter of opinion, right?

Director: You know what niceness is?

Youth: I do.

Director: And so you know when someone's being nice to you?

Youth: Of course.

Director: So if a person isn't nice to you, you'd also know?

Youth: I would.

Director: Can others see when someone isn't nice to you?

Youth: They can.

Director: Do they need proofs or do they simply see?

Youth: They simply see. But you would need to offer proof to those who haven't seen.

Father: Suppose that no one's seen. And then suppose the one who isn't nice to you is nice to everybody else.

Youth: Well, that would make me wonder why he isn't nice to me.

Director: Perhaps he doesn't like the truth, and you're aware of it while all the others aren't.

Youth: You mean he isn't strong enough for truth? And so he isn't strong enough for me? In other words, if he can't handle truth, and I declare the truth, it's likely that he won't be nice to me? So what am I to do?

Father: You speak the truth — judiciously.

Youth: You mean I have to pick and choose when I speak truth.

Father: That's right. Remember when you told Director that at times you need to hide the full extent of what you think?

Youth: I do.

Father: Just give a thought to who you're talking to. Should you come out and tell your teacher that he isn't nice, because that is the truth?

Youth: I take your point. But let's suppose I do. What comes of it? The teacher has to know he isn't nice to me. And he has got to know I know he isn't nice to me. So why not tell the truth? Am I just trying to avoid a confrontation, Dad?

Father: That is exactly what you're trying to do.

Youth: But why?

Father: Because you simply have to live with certain things, put up with them.

Youth: I don't believe that's true.

Father: In school, it's true.

Youth: Well, does it change in college, then? Can I speak freely there?

Father: If you speak freely all the time, you'll always be in confrontations, Youth. You can't fight every battle on your way. You have to choose your fight. And that's the way it is for everyone.

Youth: But what if someone picks a fight with me? Do I just walk away?

Father: At times you do. At times you fight.

Youth: But how do I know when for each?

Father: I wish I had an easy answer.

Youth: I believe you simply must resist.

Father: You're absolutely right. You must resist. But there are times when you must walk away, the times when your resistance is for naught.

Youth: Resistance never is for naught.

Father: I don't agree.

Youth: I know that you're concerned about my getting into fights. But you must know resistance doesn't always lead to fights. You just resist, and come what may.

Father: Director, can you help me here?

Director: I think that Youth has got a point. Resistance doesn't always lead to fights. The other side will often back right down. Not everybody wants a fight.

Father: But what of those who do?

Director: Why, they will start a fight regardless if you push them back or not. You might as well push back.

Father: But still, you have to choose where you will make a stand.

Director: But you don't always have that choice.

Father: You do when it is possible to run away and live to fight another day.

Director: You mean, for instance, when you're hopelessly outnumbered, right?

Father: Exactly so. And I believe that it takes strength to run in such a case.

Youth: You think that it takes strength? But how?

Father: For someone who is very proud, it would take strength to overcome that pride — prudential strength.

Youth: But is it ever really prudent to put down your pride?

Father: I wouldn't say you put it down. I'd say your prudence reins it in.

Youth: And so you have to break your pride the way you would a horse?

Father: Well, maybe "break" is not the proper word — but, yes.

Youth: And how do you do that?

Father: Through strength of reasoning. You reason with your pride until it comes around.

Youth: But you know pride. It doesn't listen very well.

Father: Then you must force your pride.

Youth: But what's to do the forcing here? What's stronger than your pride?

Father: Your mind.

Youth: But isn't pride a part of mind?

Father: Your pride is in your heart.

Youth: And so you'd have me go against my heart?

Director: What makes your pride not want to run?

Youth: To run would make you cowardly.

Father: But who would say you're cowardly?

Youth: Why, anyone.

Father: You think they'll say you're cowardly because you ran away from many boys? That's just not reasonable, Youth.

Youth: Who says that reason is involved in things like this?

Director: What is the opposite of reason?

Youth: Madness, right?

Father: Your reputation with the mad is what you care about?

Youth: I'd say you ought to care about your reputation with the sane.

Father: And isn't it insanity to stand and fight against a dozen boys?

Youth: I guess.

Father: Can you see how it is the mad who'd fault you if you run away from that?

Youth: I can.

Father: Would you be proud to have repute among the mad?

Youth: I have to say I wouldn't, no.

Director: It seems we've reasoned to your pride.

Youth: Perhaps my pride is weak.

Director: But you're the one who stood up for the truth today. Did that take pride?

Youth: I think it did.

Director: And what's your reputation now?

Youth: Among the sane? I think they think I'm brave, if just a little nuts.

Director: Among the mad?

Youth: They think that I'm a fool.

Director: With them you either are a fool to stand, or cowardly to run away? It seems you just can't win.

Youth: You can't.

Director: Now, what about the sane? Suppose you ran away.

Youth: I think that they could understand it if I did.

Director: But what exactly would they understand?

Youth: The risk of standing up for truth.

Director: The sane all know the truth?

Youth: That is the definition of their sanity.

Director: The mad don't know the truth?

Youth: They don't accept the truth.

Director: You mean they might suspect what's true?

Youth: I think they often do, but block it out.

Director: And they can't stand when others let it in?

Youth: That's right.

Director: So then the mad can't stand the sane. But do the sane all stand up for the truth?

Youth: I wish they would.

Director: Why don't they, Youth?

Youth: I guess they're cowardly.

Director: Now, when you stood up for the truth today, you were defending all the sane, because you were defending what is true, and all the sane have got an interest in the true. Do you agree?

Youth: I do. But I don't think they all appreciate what I have done.

Director: Why do you think that is?

Youth: Because a coward can't appreciate when someone else is brave.

Director: And cowards do disservice to the truth, and all the ones who know and live the truth?

Youth: They do.

Director: Does this disservice make it harder to be one with truth?

Youth: Of course it does — for all of us.

Father: But how?

Youth: It's harder to stand up for truth when you're the only one.

Director: Because you have to break the ice?

Youth: You do — and breaking ice is hard.

Father: But isn't it much better if you melt the ice instead?

Youth: With what? The gentle application of the truth?

Father: Why not?

Youth: What kind of patience would that take?

Father: A great amount. Can you be proud for being patient, Youth?

Youth: I can't be proud to be a fool.

Director: You think that only fools attempt to melt the ice?

Youth: It all depends upon the ice. If it is really thick, if it is arctic ice in winter time, the sun itself won't melt it through.

23

Director: This metaphor of breaking ice, does it seem strong or weak?

Youth: Well, it seems strong to me.

Director: What makes it strong? Resemblance to the truth?

Youth: Of course.

Director: And what about a metaphor that lies persuasively? Is that not strong if in a different way?

Youth: It is. And you must fight a metaphor like that.

Director: That's even if you have to be the one to break the ice?

Youth: That's right.

Father: You try to break the ice regardless of how strong it is in people's minds?

Youth: Regardless of how strong.

Father: And how do you do this?

Youth: You offer up the truth.

Father: And if they don't appreciate the truth?

Youth: You settle on a metaphor that is much closer to the truth than what they have in mind.

Father: And if they don't appreciate this metaphor?

Youth: There's little we can do.

Director: Now, Youth, I'm wondering. What sort of truth will we employ in our attempt to break the ice, in our attempt upon the lie?

Youth: What sort of truth?

Director: Why, yes. I mean, is there not truth that touches on external things, and then there is the truth that touches on our inner selves?

Youth: There is.

Director: And that which touches on the inner things, is that the sort of truth we use to fight the lie?

Youth: That truth is no one's business but our own, and those who're close to us.

Director: So if a person who is close to us is taken by a lie, we're free to use our inner truth to help him come around?

Youth: I think that's fair to say.

Director: And what about the others who're persuaded by a lie, the others who're not close to us? What sort of truth is left to speak about with them?

Youth: Why, many truths.

Director: But not the most important sort? Or is our inner truth not most important, friend?

Youth: No, I believe it is.

Director: And so we'll know when we can share our inner truth, just let me ask — what makes a person close to us?

Youth: Our love.

Director: And when we love, we share?

Youth: Of course.

Director: Do you believe it's true that we can only love the ones who're capable of comprehending what we have inside?

Youth: No, I don't think that's true. I mean, what if you love a child who's too young to comprehend?

Director: Well, in that case you'd only share what seems appropriate?

Youth: You would.

Director: And don't you think that it's the same with people your own age?

Youth: I think that's true — and with the older ones, as well. Not everyone can comprehend each facet of our inner truth.

Director: If that's the case, then we require privacy — I mean, for when we don't completely share?

Youth: We do.

Director: Now let's suppose another's inner truth is compromised by what is false, regardless if it's through a metaphor or not. Do we attack that lie?

Youth: I think we must.

Director: But do we violate this person's privacy in doing so?

Youth: I think we try to coax the lie on out, right to the surface, so it isn't private any more.

Director: And then?

Youth: And then we show the person it's a lie.

Director: And that will be the end of that?

Youth: That's what I like to think.

Director: But maybe we're forgetting something here. Could we be focused on the half and not the whole?

Youth: What do you mean?

Director: I mean, is it enough to simply show that something is a lie? Does that create a sort of vacuum into which the truth must rush?

Youth: You have a point. It's not enough. We have to demonstrate the truth.

Director: And if we don't?

Youth: The person might grow filled with what is false again. Or worse, he might grow filled with bitterness and mockery along with what is false.

Director: So how are we to demonstrate the truth?

Youth: We have to know exactly where the person is once he has lost his lie, and then we go to him. We go to him in gentleness and only speak the truth.

Director: To go to him, it helps to understand the lie that he once lived?

Youth: It does.

Director: Well, how do we do that?

Youth: We use imagination, right?

Father: Or else we've lived the lie ourselves and know it very well.

Youth: Have you lived lies?

Father: I'm not ashamed to tell you, Youth. I've lived a few.

Youth: And you, Director?

Director: I'm afraid I'm living lies that I don't even know are lies.

Youth: How would you know?

Director: It sometimes isn't possible to know it on your own. At times you must rely upon your friends.

Youth: To speak the truth to you.

Director: Indeed.

Youth: Because they love the truth?

Father: Because they love their friend and know the truth is good for him.

Youth: Director, do you think I'm living lies?

Director: I think you're free of many lies that other people live. Do you believe you're living lies?

Youth: I like to think I'm not. But I want you to tell me if you think I am.

Director: And I want you to tell the same to me.

Youth: I will. But I don't think you're living lies. I think the opposite.

Director: You think I live the truth? Well, why?

Youth: It's in your eyes.

Director: My eyes?

Youth: Your gaze is steady when you speak.

Director: But don't you know that certain liars hold their gazes steady, too?

Youth: It isn't just your gaze. It's what you say.

Director: And what exactly do I say?

Youth: You're always saying things that resonate.

Director: That resonate with truth?

Youth: Of course.

Director: But what if what I say is just a pleasing lie?

Youth: Well, if it resonates with me, it's resonating with a lie that I believe.

Director: The problem is you have to know the truth to feel the resonance of truth?

Youth: You do. The truth will only resonate with truth.

Director: And what if there is more to know than just the truth?

Youth: What do you mean?

Director: I mean, suppose you have to know the way, as well.

Youth: The way?

Director: Why, don't you think that there are different ways of sharing truth?

Youth: Of course I do.

Director: So if you'd like to feel that truth you have to know or understand the way a person shares.

Youth: That makes good sense.

Father: But I'm not sure what we are saying here. You mean a certain man might share his truth in treatises; another man might share his truth in oral tales?

Director: That's right, my friend. But there are ways within these ways, as well. Now let's suppose we meet a man who has a funny way of telling truth, a way that we have never come across before. Do we believe it's possible his truth might fail to resonate with us?

Youth: Assuming that we know the truth, and that he's really telling truth? It's possible.

Director: But what if he has said a thing or two that sparks our curiosity?

Youth: We'll want to learn his way.

Director: You mean to say that we won't take the easy way?

Youth: What way is that?

Director: We simply judge as soon as something fails to resonate.

Youth: We won't do that.

Director: We'll give his truth the time and effort that it needs?

Youth: We will.

Director: And what if certain people want to force this man to tell his truth another way?

Youth: We'll know that they are really after something else than truth.

Father: Agreed. But here's the thing. How do we know when it is time to stop? There's only so much time and energy that we can give to knowing this man's way. What if he is deliberately obscure, or even contradictory?

Youth: We only stop when we're no longer curious, when we have satisfied our curiosity.

Director: And that might only be when we have fully grasped his way?

Youth: Of course.

Director: But as we strive to learn his way, and even once we have, we're well aware that there are different ways?

Youth: We are.

Director: Now, if we come to grasp a number of these ways, do you believe we'll see that different ways of truth result in different types of resonance?

Youth: No, resonance is resonance. It comes from truth, not ways. What changes is how strong it is.

Director: What happens when it's fairly weak?

Youth: You feel it as a tingling on the skin.

Director: And when it's very strong?

Youth: You feel it in the marrow of your bones.

Father: We, all of us, would feel it in the marrow of our bones?

Youth: No, only those who are prepared.

Father: Prepared? I'd put it differently. I think that there are different truths for different sorts of men.

Director: You mean that there are truths for evil men and truths for those who're good?

Father: I do.

Youth: But what about the universal truth?

Father: The only universal is the truth for those with marrow like your own.

Youth: And what about our shared humanity?

Father: Do you believe that what is true for evil men is true for you? Do you believe that what is true for you is true for them?

Youth: I guess I don't. But tell me more.

Father: Well, what about the feeling that you have for your good friends. Do evil men feel that?

Youth: No, I don't think they do.

Father: That feeling is a truth that's just for us — and those like us.

Director: And those like us. Now, who exactly is like us?

Father: The strong in friendship are.

Director: The strong in friendship are the good?

Father: Of course.

Director: The good all treat their friends like gold, reciprocating any good they get?

Father: Emphatically.

Director: And if you were to sum things up, what would you say such friendship brings?

Father: It brings you peace. It brings you strength. It brings you joy.

24

Director: These things the friendship brings, do they just come all on their own or must you work for them?

Youth: I think you have to work for them

Director: You work for them together with your friend?

Youth: Of course.

Director: Well, now you've answered something I was wondering. I wondered if you thought it possible for someone else to help another gain in strength. I thought that you might say he has to do it on his own.

Youth: No, I believe it's possible to help.

Director: And these good friends, do they both find their strength at once?

Youth: Not necessarily.

Director: Well then, regardless if they come to strength together or at separate times, what do they do when they have got it, Youth?

Youth: They have to learn to exercise their strength.

Director: Do they do that alone or can each friend both guide and offer some encouragement?

Youth: It's possible to guide and offer some encouragement.

Director: Now what of peace and joy? They work for them together as with strength?

Youth: I think they do.

Director: And when they're found, what then?

Youth: It's different than with strength. We don't say that you exercise your peace, or exercise your joy.

Director: What do we do with them?

Youth: We just enjoy them, right?

Director: You mean that peace and joy have got no power of their own, a power that we use?

Youth: No, strength is where the power is.

Director: And if we use this power properly, can we find peace and joy?

Youth: I think that's how it works.

Director: Do you believe the proper use of strength must necessarily bring peace and joy?

Father: If only it would work that way.

Director: Why wouldn't it? The evil ones?

Father: If not the evil ones, then merely circumstance.

Director: The stars are not aligned?

Father: Precisely so.

Youth: But you can overcome the stars.

Father: I don't see how. The stars are luck. Your luck is simply what it is.

Director: And you must live your luck?

Father: Of course.

Director: You know that there are those who think that they can overcome their luck.

Father: And they are fools. You must adapt to luck, not try to force it, friend.

Director: What happens if you try to force your luck?

Father: That's when things get quite bad.

Director: Get bad? But why?

Father: Because your luck will not be forced. The more you force the worse it gets.

Director: You mean you'll have no peace or joy?

Father: Exactly so.

Director: So peace and joy take luck.

Father: Of course they do.

Director: It doesn't matter how much strength you have?

Father: You can't force luck, no matter how much strength you have.

Youth: So you would rather have good luck than strength?

Father: Oh, no. You must have both.

Director: You need your strength to take advantage of your luck?

Father: You do. If you have only one of them you're lost.

Director: The luck is just the opportunity to use the strength.

Father: That's right.

Director: So would you say it's luck to have your fight? I mean, you have to use your strength for that.

Father: I think that it depends upon the fight.

Youth: Well, what about the fight for truth? You always have this fight.

Father: And so we always have good luck? I don't think that's the way it works. Besides, a never ending fight would mean that there's no peace at any time.

Youth: I think it's possible to find an inner peace while in the fight for truth — the calm within the storm.

Director: And you'll find joy within this calm, as well?

Youth: You will. You'll feel the joy of victory.

Father: You honestly believe that it's good luck to have to fight for truth?

Youth: I do.

Father: But what exactly is your fight? We know that it's for truth in general terms. But what specifically?

Director: Your father's right to ask. We know you'll make a stand. But over what? Just any truth?

Youth: Not over any truth.

Director: You'll only stand for the important truths?

Youth: That's right.

Director: You mean like whether someone's heart is true?

Youth: For instance, yes.

Director: And what about the opposite, that someone's heart is false? Will you stand up for that?

Youth: I will. The truth about a rotten heart must reach the light of day.

Director: And the attention that you give it is the light of day?

Youth: It's not just my attention here. But yes, attention is the light of day — the only light these darkened hearts will ever see.

Director: The dark and false are one?

Youth: Of course they are.

Director: Suppose you have a precious truth that you hold close. Is it not dark for those with whom you do not share?

Youth: It is.

Director: And is it false?

Youth: Of course it's not.

Director: So how do you determine whether something's truly false, and not just dark because it isn't shared? In other words, how do you find your fight?

Youth: I guess I have to get to know the one in question.

Director: You must win his trust?

Youth: But what if he has got a rotten heart? Then I don't want his trust.

Director: Do you believe that there are signs you'll see, without his trust, to tell you whether he has got a rotten heart?

Youth: I do.

Director: What are these signs?

Youth: You'll see them in his acts, in whether he is hurting others, right?

Director: And if he's helping others we assume his heart is good?

Youth: If he is truly helping, yes.

Director: A man like that, you'd like to win his trust?

Youth: I would.

Director: You'd like to win it so he tells you what he holds so dear?

Youth: That's not the only reason, but it's true I'd like to know.

Director: But let's suppose he doesn't want to tell.

Youth: Well, I'd respect his privacy.

Director: Not everybody would.

Youth: I know. But if he's good he has good reason why he doesn't want to let me in.

Director: And you can live with that?

Youth: I can.

Director: Do you believe the good who hold their precious secrets tight are strong?

Youth: Of course. A secret's not an easy thing to keep.

Director: Do rotten men have secrets, too?

Youth: They do.

Director: And do they hold them tight?

Youth: I think they do.

Director: Does this mean they are strong?

Youth: I guess.

Director: So strength in secrecy alone can't tell you if a man is good or bad?

Youth: That's true.

Director: You have to know what sort of man you're dealing with.

Youth: You do.

Director: And you can tell from what he does.

Youth: You can.

Director: But let's suppose you are not witness to the things he does. Is there another way to tell what sort of man he is?

Youth: I think there is. A good man has a sort of glow.

Director: A glow from fire lit deep down inside?

Youth: That's right.

Director: The rotten man has got no fire in his soul?

Youth: He's dead inside.

Director: What does it take to light the fire, Youth?

Youth: Integrity. You cannot truly live without integrity.

Director: And you can recognize the living from the dead at once?

Youth: Well, maybe not at once. It's best to watch the things they do.

Director: Because the glow might come from something else?

Youth: It might.

Director: What else could cause a glow?

Youth: Reflected light?

Director: You have a point. But if a person has that certain inner glow, and when you watch his deeds you see that he is true, can you be sure he has integrity?

Youth: You can.

Director: Can everybody recognize integrity, the living and the dead?

Youth: I think they can.

Director: And everyone can recognize the opposite?

Youth: They can.

Director: If everyone can recognize the two, then why are people often fooled?

Youth: You mean that someone sees integrity where there is none?

Director: Or just the opposite.

Youth: They must be blind.

Director: Because of what?

Youth: I couldn't say.

Father: Perhaps it is because they're thinking wishfully.

Youth: You mean when someone likes to think a rotten man has got integrity.

Father: Of course. But it is also wishful thought when someone likes to think a man of great integrity is rotten in his core.

Youth: But why would someone think a man like that is bad inside?

Father: Perhaps the rotten can't believe that everyone is not, deep down inside, like them.

Youth: They must assume that everyone is truly weak. That's sad.

Director: If you were weak, my friend, would you believe that others could be strong?

Youth: I would, because my eyes can see the truth.

Director: But don't you think that it takes strength to see the truth?

Youth: I think the truth, concerning certain things, is clear to everyone, regardless of their strength.

Director: And yet we still find people who can't see?

Youth: Well, maybe everyone can see, but sometimes they don't use their eyes.

Director: What do they use instead?

Youth: Their wills.

Director: You mean they force the facts?

Youth: I do.

Director: You mean they shove the round into the square?

Youth: They do.

Director: Well, that won't do. Why do you think they shove?

Youth: Impatience likes to force the facts.

Director: But forcing facts will lead to what?

Youth: Abomination.

Director: My, that's quite a word.

Youth: But I believe that it's appropriate.

Director: What other way is there to turn the truth into abomination, Youth?

Youth: You break it up. A partial truth will season any lie.

Director: So there are chefs of truth?

Youth: I'd rather say that there are chefs of lies.

Director: That's fine. The base ingredient's the lie?

Youth: Of course.

Father: What if the base ingredient's the truth?

Youth: And it is seasoned with a lie? Why would you season truth with lies?

Father: Perhaps you wish to make the truth more palatable, Youth.

Youth: I wouldn't like the way it tastes.

Father: You like it pure. Not everybody does.

Youth: So we should spice things up for them?

25

Director: Suppose we serve the food in purest form. What is the worst that happens then?

Father: A number of our guests won't like the taste.

Youth: But truth is good for them.

Father: But they won't eat this truth. And they'll go off and get some junk to fill them up instead. You'd rather they do that than have us spice the truth for them?

Youth: But can't the spice be other truths that will enhance, not mask, the flavor of the basic truth?

Father: If you enhance the flavor of a thing that someone doesn't like you only make it worse.

Youth: Then maybe we should only serve the ones who like the taste. Forget the rest. They don't deserve the unadulterated truth.

Director: And when we serve the ones who like the taste, will we serve all our truths, our every truth?

Youth: You mean our inner truths, as well? I'm not so sure. Some things you just don't share with simply anyone.

Director: But is it merely anyone who can appreciate your truth?

Youth: I guess you have a point. But still . . .

Director: Some things you share, some things you don't? But when you share it's pure?

Youth: Exactly, yes.

Director: And there is risk when sharing inner truths?

Youth: There is.

Director: Suppose you know — you know from evidence, experiments, from facts — a thing you keep inside to be the truth. And then suppose you tell a friend this truth, and he denies it's true. What do you do?

Youth: I try to make him come around.

Director: But if you can't?

Youth: I guess we must agree to disagree.

Director: Would he remain your friend?

Youth: I think he would.

Director: Would he remain your confidant?

Youth: I guess.

Director: With confidants you share your inner truths, correct?

Youth: Correct.

Director: Let's say that you have seven inner truths. Your confidant knows three. He's fine with two, but he objects to one. He doesn't think it's true, despite what you are telling him. Would you go on to share the other four?

Youth: I guess I would, but I'd proceed more cautiously.

Director: Because if someone balks at truth it's likely that he'll balk again?

Youth: I think that's so. It's only natural to be more cautious after that.

Director: Would you feel wounded, Youth?

Youth: In truth? I would. And you, Director?

Director: Me? I'd use it as an opportunity to verify my truth. I must assume it's possible my friend is right, no matter all my certainty.

Youth: I think that you should share an inner truth with us.

Director: What makes you think I haven't, Youth?

Youth: You've shared an inner truth today?

Director: I have — if not, however, in so many words.

Youth: Please put it in so many words.

Director: This inner truth is called philosophy.

Youth: But why is that an inner truth?

Director: Because I do not have discussions like the one we've had today with simply anyone.

Youth: Discussions of the truth are not for everyone, agreed. But . . .

Director: Yes?

Youth: But now that we have talked, do you believe they are... for me?

Director: That's something you'll decide all on your own.

Youth: And if they're not?

Director: There's nothing wrong with that.

Youth: I want to be... like you.

Director: And like your father, too?

Youth: Of course!

Father: But I am no philosopher, though I admit I'm often taken with philosophy.

Youth: But you're an honest man.

Father: I try to be, at any rate.

Youth: Well, you succeed. And that's philosophy enough.

Father: Director, too, is honest, Youth. And there is much that you can learn from him.

Youth: Because you think that I'm not honest, Dad?

Father: Oh, no! Because I think Director has a certain strength that you'd do well to learn.

Youth: The strength of his philosophy.

Father: Exactly so.

Youth: So we have been philosophizing here today?

Director: We have. Perhaps philosophy is in the cards for you.

Youth: But what if I'm not strong enough?

Director: You show some signs of strength.

Youth: You really think I do?

Director: Do you believe I'd lie about a thing like that?

Youth: I'm sorry. No.

Director: Your father thinks philosophy might be your thing.

Youth: You spoke of this?

Father: We did. And we agreed that you should spend more time in conversation with Director, Youth.

Youth: I'd like that, very much.

Father: I thought you would.

Youth: But I can talk about the truth with you, you know.

Father: Oh, I expect you will. But I believe you need more help than I can give.

Youth: More help? You think there's something wrong with me?

Father: Why, no — the opposite!

Youth: I really do appreciate this, Dad.

Father: I only ask that you make good your time. You'll meet Director once a week. He is your tutor now.

Youth: You're paying him?

Father: He won't accept a penny for his work with you.

Youth: So I'm a charity?

Director: You're hardly that. It is my pleasure to engage with you in talk.

Youth: So we'll just talk?

Director: That's right.

Youth: I think that this sounds great! What will we talk about?

Director: Why, anything and everything — but mostly we'll discuss what's happening at school.

Youth: Well, that will give us much to talk about. But can we talk about what's happening with you?

Director: Of course.

Youth: You think I'm old enough?

Director: You certainly are old enough.

Youth: Why, thanks. But will it be a one way street?

Director: You mean will I help you with nothing in return? I told you, Youth. I will enjoy our talks.

Youth: And that's the only reason that you'll meet with me?

Father: Well, maybe he'll recruit you to the cause.

Youth: You mean philosophy.

Father: Indeed.

Youth: Do you recruit a lot of boys?

Director: No, you would be the first.

Youth: The first? You're serious?

Director: I am.

Youth: Then you don't really know if I am right for this.

Director: That's true.

Father: But he would like to take the chance.

Youth: Suppose I don't live up to what you hope.

Director: What do you think I hope? We'll have a pleasant time, and maybe learn a thing or two. And that's enough. But if there's more, if you take up philosophy all on your own, that's nice.

Youth: It's only nice?

Director: What can I say? It would be nice.

Youth: So where do we begin?

Director: By finishing what we're about today.

Youth: And what is that? Attempting to encourage me so I feel strong?

Director: Why, no. We are attempting to encourage you to tap your strength.

Youth: You know that I have strength?

Director: I know that you have strength.

Youth: What makes you say?

Director: My gut and mind.

Youth: I wish my gut and mind told me the same. Do yours tell you that you are strong?

Director: My actions tell my gut and mind that I am strong.

Youth: What do you do?

Director: I mostly talk. Or don't you think that talk is action, Youth?

Youth: I'm sure it can be, yes.

Director: But sometimes it is not?

Youth: It's not when nothing comes of it.

Father: The trick is making something come of it.

Youth: I'd like to learn that trick.

Director: I'll do my best to teach it to you, then — assuming that you don't already know, and that it's possible to teach a thing like this. But tell me, now. What sort of consequences do you want your acts to have?

Youth: What sort? The sort that help the good.

Director: And can you guess the way to help the good?

Youth: To speak the truth? To speak in favor of the truth?

Director: And which of these is best? To speak in favor of the truth, or speak the truth itself?

Youth: To speak the truth itself.

Director: Do you believe it takes more strength to speak the truth than just to speak about the truth?

Youth: Of course it does. But both are good.

Director: And why is that?

Youth: It's obvious why speaking truth is good. But when you speak in favor of the truth, you lend support.

Director: Now tell me why support is good.

Youth: It can encourage others to articulate the truth.

Director: And truth, is it a catalyst?

Youth: It is. It's as we've said. It drives away the false.

Director: And as the false is driven out it's easier and easier to speak the truth?

Youth: I think it is.

Director: And in the end we all would speak the truth? Is that the goal?

Youth: Supposing that it's not impossible? I think that is a noble goal.

Director: And what about our inner truths?

Youth: If everyone is speaking truth, impossible as that may be, I don't believe that inner truths are needed any more. In other words, we need not hide the truth. But that's a long way off.

Director: Indeed. But you will aim toward that end, impossible as it may be?

Youth: I will.

Director: How much support do you believe you'll gain if you intend to rid the world of inner truth?

Youth: That's just the final step. It makes no sense unless the whole world's speaking truth.

Director: Because if everyone is speaking truth then everyone is worthy of our trust?

Youth: Exactly so.

Director: So trust is based on truth?

Youth: Of course.

Director: Suppose the evil speak the truth.

Youth: What makes them evil, then?

Director: The other things they do.

Youth: But if they're doing evil things they'll have to lie.

Director: Because the truthful won't put up with them, their evil deeds?

Youth: That's right. They'll have to hide those deeds with lies.

Director: Suppose that in this brave new world of truth some people do a deed to you that you don't like, but everybody else just thinks it's fine, so no one feels compelled to lie. Will you speak up?

Youth: I will.

Director: Despite the fact that everybody disagrees with you?

Youth: I like to think I'd speak the truth.

Director: The truth that you did not appreciate the deed.

Youth: That's right.

Director: You're speaking of the things you like or do not like, correct?

Youth: Correct.

Director: And everyone should speak the truth about the things they like or do not like?

Youth: The world would be a simpler place.

Director: In many ways I think it would. What stops us now from speaking what we feel? Are we not strong enough?

Youth: Perhaps. But I believe the problem is it's often wise, the way things are today, to hold your tongue.

26

Director: But what is wisdom, Youth?

Youth: What's best for you.

Director: At times it's best to speak? At times it's best to hold your tongue?

Youth: That's right. In either case you can be wise.

Director: And how are you to know when it is time for which?

Youth: You listen to your gut and mind.

Director: What happens then? One person might decide to speak? Another just might clam right up? Despite the fact the circumstances are the same?

Youth: I guess.

Director: And if each one obeys his gut and mind, then both are wise?

Youth: But can the circumstances really be the same? Each person's circumstances are unique.

Director: Shall we distinguish circumstances here? There are the circumstances of the scene, and then there are the circumstances of the man, the circumstances that he brings into the scene?

Youth: I think that's right.

Director: And do the circumstances of the scene require certain sorts of acts?

Youth: The scene itself requires certain sorts of acts? You mean that there's a sort of logic to the scene?

Director: I do.

Youth: Well, I believe that's true. It's what's expected, right?

Director: It's what the scene demands. Suppose you are a man who comes upon this scene, and it feels right, deep down within your gut, and mind makes no objections here. You'll act within the scene and you'll be wise as long as you are in alignment with your gut and mind, with how you feel and think.

Youth: And that's not fair.

Director: Because another man will come along and feel and think that it's all wrong?

Youth: Exactly, yes.

Director: And what is wise for him?

Youth: He must denounce the scene.

Director: Denounce the scene? Despite the fact that it seems good for others, Youth?

Youth: Despite the fact.

Director: If everyone is being wise it seems we're in for conflict, yes?

Youth: I guess we are.

Director: Are you alright with that?

Youth: I have to be. It's just a fact. Not every scene is meant for everyone.

Director: Would this be so if everyone were speaking truth?

Youth: It would, if they are speaking truth for them.

Director: The truth for them. Do you believe there is a higher truth, a truth for everyone?

Youth: I like to think there is.

Director: But you're not sure.

Youth: I'm not. Perhaps there only is for certain things.

Director: You don't mean things that people like.

Youth: No, that's the preference of the individual.

Director: Your preferences must be unique?

Youth: That's right. They have to be — if you're to be an individual.

Director: I thought you'd say the individual is what he says and does.

Youth: Your words and acts derive from preferences.

Director: And preferences derive from gut and mind?

Youth: They do.

Director: But what if you don't listen to your mind or gut?

Youth: Then preferences must come from somewhere else.

Director: But where?

Youth: I guess it has to be the minds and guts of others, no?

Director: But how would someone know what's in the minds and guts of others, Youth?

Youth: The others speak and act.

Director: And this is how we get the scene?

Youth: The greater part of it, at least.

Director: And so the scene demands, and certain people simply acquiesce, despite the fact it's really not for them?

Youth: That's how it is.

Director: But they should really speak and act against the scene?

Youth: That's how it ought to be.

Director: But they are weak?

Youth: I know that they are weak.

Director: What would it take for them to gain in strength, in confidence?

Youth: Good friends would help.

Director: And with these friends they're strong enough to challenge any scene?

Youth: That's right.

Director: And what is best? To fit the scene?

Youth: I think that's easiest.

Director: But if you fit the scene, the scene has claims on you. And you must live those claims.

Youth: That's true. Do you believe it's easier to fight the scene?

Director: I'm not sure which is easier.

Youth: Which one is best?

Director: Which one is best for me?

Youth: Which one is simply best?

Director: It doesn't work that way.

Youth: Each one of us decides what's best?

Director: That's right.

Youth: Director, if you tell yourself it's best for you to fight the scene, then why not simply tell yourself and others, too, that it's the simple truth for all?

Director: Because it's not.

Youth: I like your honesty.

Director: If it seems good to you to fight the scene, then fight. If it seems good to you to join the scene, then you should join.

Youth: I wish I had your equanimity.

Director: Don't get me wrong. I am opposed to scenes that I don't like.

Youth: But there are scenes you like?

Director: There are. I sometimes visit them.

Youth: But you do not belong?

Director: That's right.

Youth: Philosophy has got a scene.

Director: Well, if it does, I think that it's a different sort of thing. It's here with us right now.

Youth: There is no larger scene?

Director: Why, there may well be other conversations going on in other places, Youth.

Youth: How many philosophic conversations do you think go on at any given time?

Director: Oh, I suppose a number do.

Youth: A number? Is that number great or small?

Director: I think that number's great, why even if it's just a few.

Youth: What happens if those few, those conversations, end?

Director: I guess the candle flickers out.

Father: You have to fight to keep the conversation going, Youth.

Youth: I know.

Director: Do you believe it's easier to fight this fight beside your friends?

Youth: I do.

Director: Because they lend support?

Youth: That's right. They stir your heart.

Director: And stirred up hearts are strong?

Youth: They are.

Director: But what about the mind?

Youth: You're worried that the heart will overcome the mind?

Director: The two should work in harmony, don't you agree?

Youth: Of course.

Director: How do you stir the mind?

Youth: Your friends can stir your mind.

Director: Am I friend like that?

Youth: You are, most certainly.

Director: And how exactly do I stir? Am I provocative?

Youth: Provocative? You speak the truth.

Director: And if the truth provokes, that's fine?

Youth: I wouldn't say that it provokes. I'd say it stirs.

Director: A stirred up mind is strong?

Youth: I think it is.

Director: As long as it's not too stirred up? As long as it's not crazy, right?

Youth: That's true enough.

Director: What makes for craziness?

Youth: When you've got nothing firm within your mind.

Director: When absolutely everything's stirred up at once?

Youth: That's right.

Director: When everything is all stirred up you're weak?

Youth: You are.

Director: You need at least a single thing that's firm within your mind?

Youth: That's right. You need a rock, a rock of strength.

Director: And this, this rock, is something that you know, you really know?

Youth: It is.

Director: But what exactly is this thing that's firm, this thing you really know?

Youth: A truth about the world?

Director: Can you say more?

Youth: I can't.

Director: Alright. But tell me this. Is it a truth about the world that truth is best? I mean, can someone really know that truth is truly best?

Youth: Of course.

Director: Not everybody knows this truth?

Youth: Well, if they do they sure don't act on it.

Director: But why? Perhaps they've had a bad experience with truth?

Youth: So they conclude it's good to lie?

Director: Don't you agree? I mean, don't you agree that they conclude it's good?

Youth: I do.

Director: Now here's the thing I'm wondering. Can lies be rocks of strength to troubled minds? Can people cling to them?

Youth: I think they can. It's possible to found your life upon a lie.

Director: But if your life is founded on a lie, what happens then?

Youth: It might collapse when things are really stirred.

Director: But if you're on a rock, then you can really stir it up and have no fear?

Youth: I think that's true.

Father: But there's a problem here. Some people found their lives on things they think are true but aren't. In other words, it's not a lie. It's simply false.

Director: Which way is better, then? The conscious lie or something false you think is true?

Youth: The latter is more honest, right?

Director: But which will stand up better in a storm?

Youth: They both will fail you when it comes to it.

Director: What sort of person founds his life upon a conscious lie?

Youth: A wretched man?

Director: What sort of person founds his life upon a thing he thinks is true but really isn't true?

Youth: A fool?

Director: You don't seem very sure.

Youth: I worry that I'm one of these.

Director: Don't worry, Youth. You're very worry means you're likely not. You know you have to verify your truths, especially your most important truth, your rock.

Youth: I do.

Director: Now, many do not verify. Would you agree?

Youth: Of course.

Director: They take their truths on faith?

Youth: They do.

Director: They think that all they have to do is just believe, and that is good enough?

Youth: That's how it is for many, yes.

Father: They just believe in what?

Youth: Themselves, let's say.

Father: What's wrong with that?

Youth: They think they're better than they are.

Director: What happens when they think they're better than they are?

Youth: They do disservice to themselves, and others, too.

Director: Disservice, how?

Youth: To others they're not fair. They think they're better than the others, when in fact they're not.

Director: And how disservice to themselves?

Youth: They never come to know themselves for what they really are.

Father: But if they're worse than what they think they are, is it a benefit to know themselves for that?

Youth: Not all at once. But over time their knowledge of themselves will make them better men.

Father: You're saying that they can't improve unless they know how bad they are?

Youth: I am.

Director: So you must know the truth, the ugly truth, before you can improve that truth, before you can improve yourself?

Youth: You must.

Director: And when you have improved yourself, you have your proper confidence? You have your rock?

Youth: That's right.

Director: But what if from the start you know the truth about yourself, you really know?

Youth: Assuming that this truth is not an ugly truth? I think that's very rare. But then you must believe that you can live your truth.

Director: But can't you know that you can live this truth, not just believe?

Youth: I guess you can.

Director: Well, let's suppose the opposite — you don't know you can live your truth.

Youth: But why?

Director: Because your truth is just an inner truth, a truth that's not yet manifest.

Youth: But can't you live an inner truth?

Director: In some sense, yes. But should the truth be kept inside, or should it see the light of day?

Youth: You mean at least among your friends?

Director: I do.

Youth: Then I believe that it should see the light of day.

Director: You have to share your latent truth to make it something more. Or have I got it wrong?

Youth: No, I believe that's true. We have to share our inner truth, whenever possible.

Director: And if it's possible just once, the truth has still been shared?

Youth: It has.

Director: But our truths, they are not meant for everyone?

Youth: They're only meant for those we love and trust.

Director: And how are we to share these truths? Can we just tell them in so many words?

Youth: It's not enough to say these truths. We have to demonstrate.

Father: But what if someone has a truth like ours, and when we try to say this truth aloud he knows exactly what we mean?

Youth: Well, maybe then it's possible to tell our truth in just so many words — but only once we've shown that it goes deeper than mere words alone.

27

Director: And do you know what else goes deeper than mere words alone?

Youth: I don't.

Director: The different types of life.

Youth: What types?

Director: Well, there's the tragic life, and there's the comic life. Now, if you had a choice, which life would you prefer?

Youth: The comic life, I'd have to say.

Director: How can you make your life a comedy?

Youth: You open up your heart and let the comic in?

Director: Supposing that you do, when you are speaking from the heart, you speak in comic terms?

Youth: You do.

Director: Then tell me how you speak in comic terms.

Youth: You speak of happy endings, right?

Director: Would you be optimistic, Youth?

Youth: I think you would.

Director: But can't the tragic soul be optimistic, too?

Youth: Unduly optimistic, yes.

Director: What makes it so?

Youth: The optimism of this soul is serious, is deadly serious.

Director: And does the comic soul have optimism with a grain of salt, a lighter touch?

Youth: It does.

Director: Now, if things don't turn out, do you believe the comic soul can deal with this much better than the tragic soul?

Youth: I do. While tragic souls are devastated, comic souls can bounce back much more easily.

Director: And all because of just that little grain of salt?

Youth: That's right.

Director: So salt must be the heart of comedy?

Youth: It is.

Director: And what's the heart of tragedy?

Youth: A lack of salt.

Director: Where do we get the salt?

Youth: We have to find it in ourselves.

Director: The tragic never look for it?

Youth: I don't believe they do.

Director: But can't the comic teach the tragic how to find their salt?

Youth: I don't think that is such an easy thing.

Director: And why is that?

Youth: Because the tragic think they know.

Director: What do they think they know?

Youth: They think they know the way of things, and don't need any salt.

Director: But they don't know?

Youth: Of course they don't.

Director: And do the comic know?

Youth: They know that they don't know the way of things, a single way of things. They know that there are many ways.

Director: And tragic men believe that comic men are fools since they are not upon the single way?

Youth: They do, Director, certainly. The single tragic way is serious. The ways of comedy are not — or not completely so.

Director: It's just that little grain of salt that makes the difference here?

Youth: Correct. At times it's even hard to tell the comic from the tragic at first glance.

Director: But can't you tell them by how flexible they are? I mean, a tragic man, so serious upon his single way, can he be loose when warranted?

Youth: You have a point. He can't.

Director: Rigidity is not a virtue, right, is not a strength?

Youth: That's right.

Director: And on the other hand, while comic souls are sometimes loose, they are not always loose, now are they, Youth? Can't they be firm, and even very firm, when it is time for that?

Youth: They can.

Director: But they are never rigid, yes?

Youth: They're not.

Director: Do you believe that they can share their salt with tragic souls?

Youth: Not when they only have a single grain.

Director: But if a man is strong in comedy, and he has many grains to spare? Can he then share?

Youth: I think that he can try. But I'm not sure that it will work.

Director: Why not?

Youth: Because it seems to me that salt is actually a metaphor for virtue. Virtue is your own, not something that is shared.

Director: What sort of virtue do you think it is?

Youth: The virtue of humanity.

Director: You don't think that the tragic have humanity?

Youth: Well, if they do it seems it's frozen up.

Director: How do you know it's frozen up?

Youth: It's in the way the tragic laugh, or don't.

Director: You have to laugh a certain way to have humanity?

Youth: Of course you do.

Director: But what's this certain way?

Youth: You know it when you hear it, right?

Director: Then are the comic laughing all the time?

Youth: No, not at all. They only laugh when something's truly funny.

Director: When is something truly funny?

Youth: When an unexpected truth comes out.

Father: That's sometimes true. But sometimes funny is, for some, buffoonery.

Director: You don't believe buffoonery can have an element of unexpected truth?

Father: Well, if it can it is an element of baser truth.

Director: Agreed. Now tell me, Youth. Is there a way to make the tragic laugh?

Youth: Well, if there is, we have to start by dealing with their lies.

Director: Their lies?

Youth: Of course. These lies are what have frozen their humanity. They go against the heart, the seat of warmth.

Director: What is the coldest sort of lie?

Youth: The sort that's closest to the truth.

Director: And why is that?

Youth: Because it's sneakiest. Because it subtly distorts the truth.

Director: And what about a brazen lie? How cold is that?

Youth: I don't think it's as cold.

Director: Because it's obviously a lie?

Youth: That's right.

Director: But what if it's not obvious to you?

Youth: Then I suppose that it's as cold as any subtle lie.

Director: Now, tell me what is worse — if you believe a lie that others tell, or tell a lie yourself.

Youth: I think they both will ice you up.

Director: So if we want to help a tragic soul we seek to stop its telling and believing lies?

Youth: That's right.

Director: We seek to change the habits of that soul?

Youth: We do.

Director: And if the habits change the soul will warm and laugh in all of its humanity?

Youth: I like to think it will.

Director: But even if it doesn't laugh just yet, it will be stronger, no?

Youth: Of course it will. A lie will always sap your strength. If you get rid of it you're stronger necessarily.

Director: And in this strength you would be proud?

Youth: Most certainly.

Director: Do you believe there ever is a time when you'd be proud to hold or tell a lie?

Youth: I don't.

Father: But what if you must lie to save yourself, or those you love, from evil men? Can't you be proud of overcoming them?

Youth: You never can be proud to use a lie as means to reach your end.

Director: You would employ the means but not be proud?

Youth: I would, if forced.

Director: And what about the ones who won't employ the necessary means? Are these not tragic souls of sorts?

Youth: If they're so rigid in their way that they can't save themselves and those they love from evil men, then yes, I'd say they're tragic. They'd be better off with proud and comic souls, the sort that can be firm, and very firm, in truth.

Director: And they'd be better still if they could save themselves by telling truth instead of being forced to lie?

Youth: Of course.

Director: Does it take strength to tell the truth?

Youth: At times it does.

Director: What times?

Youth: When it is inconvenient.

Director: Those who lie when it's convenient, they are weak?

Youth: Of course they are.

Director: Regardless if it is a brazen or a subtle lie?

Youth: That's right.

Father: And what about the ones who lie when it is inconvenient, are they strong?

Youth: When is it inconvenient to tell lies?

Father: When truth would be much easier.

Youth: Then why not tell the truth?

Father: Because the truth might hurt.

Youth: But truth is truth. We have to tell the truth.

Father: Regardless if it hurts a friend?

Youth: A friend who's worth his salt would want the truth.

Father: But can't we bide our time until we find a gentle way to say what must be said?

Youth: But sometimes truth is needed urgently.

Father: In that case we would tell it right away, and come what may. But when it isn't needed urgently, do you believe that inconvenient lies take strength?

Youth: I'll tell you what is wrong with this. We only lie to enemies. It's never right to lie to friends.

Director: And are we strong when lying to an enemy?

Youth: We're not. We have to lie to enemies because we're weak, precisely that.

Director: The weakness justifies the lie?

Youth: I hate to say it does, but yes.

Director: What does it mean to justify?

Youth: To show that something's right — or rather, that it isn't wrong.

Director: And if you're very weak in many things you'd have to tell a great amount of lies, and you'd be justified?

Youth: Well, that's the thing. The lies become an awful sort of crutch. You must stand up for truth, despite the fact that you're attacked by enemies.

Director: Unless the threat is very serious?

Youth: But even then you tell the truth if possible. The lie must truly be your last resort.

Director: So even those who're weak must stand up to the vast majority of threats?

Youth: That's right.

Director: Do you have strength enough to stand up to the vast majority of threats?

Youth: I like to think I do.

Director: How did you get that strength?

Youth: From practice standing up.

Director: So that's the way that you'd advise the weak to gain in strength? They have to practice standing up?

Youth: Of course.

Director: And do they start quite small and work their way on up?

Youth: That way seems best.

Father: But what if all the threats they face are large? How can they ever start?

Youth: I guess they can't. They're stuck. And that is very sad.

Director: But can we help?

Youth: But how? They have to learn to stand up on their own. It does no good if we are always standing up for them. They'll be annihilated when they're on their own again.

Director: And so it's simply sad, with nothing to be done?

Youth: Perhaps the weak can band together to defend themselves.

Director: They'll always stay together so they're not alone?

Youth: That's right. They'll help each other fight.

Director: Well, that might work. But you don't want to be a part of that?

Youth: I like to stand up on my own.

Director: Because you're strong.

Youth: I am.

Director: But you would help the weak if opportunity arose?

Youth: Of course I would. But I don't want to band with them.

Director: Because they'll bring you down?

Youth: I'm not ashamed to say that's true.

Director: There's nothing wrong with that. You'll help them when you can. And your example might be good for them. If they grow stronger, some of them might want to stand alone.

Father: Is that the end of strength, to stand alone?

Youth: I think at times you have to stand alone. But then at times you need to stand with friends.

Father: And how do you know when it's time for which?

Youth: You have to listen to your mind and gut. At times your friends are right. At times your friends are wrong. You stand with them when they are right. When they are wrong you try to help them see. And if they do not come to see, you stand alone.

28

Director: So we can help the weak but not be one of them?

Youth: That's right.

Director: But do we risk ourselves in doing so?

Youth: At times I think we do.

Director: And when is it appropriate to risk ourselves?

Youth: When there's a chance for us to make a difference.

Director: By putting off what would have happened had we not stepped in?

Youth: That's right. We're buying time.

Director: In hopes of what?

Youth: In hopes the weak will gain in strength.

Director: And throw the evil off themselves?

Youth: Exactly so.

Director: Suppose we buy a lot of time and still the weak are weak, and cannot throw the evil off.

Youth: Then maybe we have bought enough. The key is knowing if they're making any progress.

Director: If the weak progress, we lend support?

Youth: We do.

Director: But if they don't we drop them right away?

Youth: Perhaps not right away, but yes. I know that it sounds cold. But there is only just so much that we can do.

Director: Unless they have some sort of claim on us?

Youth: You mean they're friends or family, right? And they're not acting in the wrong? I take your point. In that case we would have to stick with them.

Director: Suppose they have no claim. And then suppose they never gain in strength but nonetheless keep getting up when they are beaten down.

Youth: They're strong in their determination?

Director: Yes. Would we support them in their fight?

Youth: You're asking if we'd back a hopeless cause?

Director: Would it be hopeless if we help them win?

Youth: It all depends. Can they sustain the victory without support from us?

Director: Let's say they can't.

Youth: Then I can't see the point.

Father: Now you surprise me, Youth. I thought you'd say the point is not to let the evil take the stage. I thought you'd say we have to drive them off, no matter what.

Youth: Well, there are many fights in life. We have to choose our battles, right?

Director: That's even when the ugly head of evil rears right up in front of you? Does that leave you a choice?

Youth: Assuming I have strength enough? I wouldn't hesitate to smash it in.

Director: In order to protect the weaker ones who're beautiful in moral terms?

Youth: That's right.

Director: The weak, are they all beautiful?

Youth: You mean do they have moral strength? Not all of them, of course. We only fight for those who do.

Director: The ugly, they lack moral strength?

Youth: Of course they do.

Director: So we are fighting for the strong against the weak?

Youth: But only when the strong are weak in other things.

Director: These other things, they are amoral, Youth?

Youth: Well, everything that strictly speaking isn't moral or immoral is amoral, right?

Director: So we have moral strength and other strengths, amoral strengths.

Youth: We do. And moral strength's the key to all the other strengths.

Director: But what about the martial arts? Is moral strength the key to them?

Youth: Well, I believe it is. You need integrity in body and in mind if you're to fight effectively.

Director: And this integrity, it's always moral strength? Can't someone be quite good in martial arts and not be beautiful in moral terms?

Youth: I guess that's possible.

Director: And so the strength of martial arts itself, and by itself, is not a moral strength. It's possible to fight effectively cut free from moral ties.

Youth: That's true. It's what the evil do.

Director: But you would learn the strength of martial arts in order to support your moral strength.

Youth: I would.

Director: And so your moral strength won't stand completely on its own. You'd have another strength supporting it, a strength that isn't strictly moral, right?

Youth: That's right. I'd put that strength to moral use.

Director: And that's the thing, the use to which you put your strengths.

Youth: Of course.

Director: Now you have yet to study martial arts. But do you think that you have other strengths, the way things are for you today?

Youth: I'd say that I have more than moral strength.

Director: And do you use these strengths to lend support to moral strength?

Youth: I do. My moral strength is in command.

Director: Do you believe it's possible to fight with moral strength alone? Or do you always need some other strength to lend support?

Youth: I think you always need some other strength, why even if it's simply stamina.

Director: What good is moral strength alone, without another strength to help it out?

Youth: It's like a general who's got no army, right?

Director: I think you put that well. The leader needs the ones he leads. Now, are we sure that moral strength should take command of all the other strengths? Or do we need to offer proof?

Youth: I think it's clear enough. But maybe we can hear the proof another time?

Director: We can, most certainly. But as things stand right now, do you agree that you must build your other strengths?

Youth: I do.

Director: And how are you to build these strengths?

Youth: For one, I have to learn to fight.

Director: With fists and otherwise?

Youth: With fists and otherwise.

Director: Now let me ask you this. If you know how to fight, are you obliged to teach the ones of moral worth who don't?

Youth: Yes, I would feel obliged.

Director: Just as the one who teaches you will feel obliged?

Youth: If he's a proper teacher, yes.

Director: This sense of obligation, do you think that it's a sign of worth?

Youth: I do.

Director: And what about integrity?

Youth: If teaching certain worthy others is a part of this man's moral code, then I would say that it's a sign of that, as well.

Director: And if you learn from someone with integrity, will he impart integrity to you?

Youth: I think he'll try.

Director: Not everyone who learns from someone with integrity is guaranteed to learn integrity himself?

Youth: That's true. But it is possible to learn integrity all on your own.

Director: And if you learned integrity all on your own, would you feel proud?

Youth: I would, and rightly so.

Director: Is it the same with all of moral strength?

Youth: I think that there are many things that you can learn from others here. But there are certain things you have to learn alone.

Director: The evil, can they learn these things?

Youth: The evil wouldn't want to learn.

Director: And why is that?

Youth: They think that only fools have moral strength.

Director: But why do they think that?

Youth: Because they can't see any good that comes of it. They think that moral strength exposes you to risk.

Director: Because their brethren evil prey upon the ones with moral strength? They seek the moral out and hope to crush them in their strength?

Youth: And they don't always have to seek them out. Some of the moral ones are itching for a fight.

Director: Do you go itching for a fight?

Youth: At times I do.

Director: And were you itching for the fight today?

Youth: Perhaps a little bit.

Director: Because you had to make a point?

Youth: That's right.

Director: You made your point. And are you happy now?

Youth: I am.

Director: Despite the fact that some will think that you're a fool?

Youth: Too bad for them.

Director: Yet you, the one they think to be a fool, are happy, right?

Youth: That's right. I mostly am.

Director: And mostly's good enough?

Youth: Well, I'd take more.

Director: What would it take for more?

Youth: More strength.

Director: Do you believe we three are strong?

Youth: I do.

Director: Do you believe that others think we're strong?

Youth: It doesn't matter what they think.

Director: You're sounding confident.

Youth: That's how I'm feeling now.

Director: Do you believe your confidence will bother ugly souls?

Youth: I think it likely will. And they can rot as far as I'm concerned.

Director: What happens when they rot?

Youth: What do you mean?

Director: I mean, do they become much better or do they grow worse?

Youth: The latter, certainly.

Director: Should we attempt to stop their growing worse?

Youth: I don't see how that's possible.

Director: Can we encourage them?

Youth: They'll only laugh.

Director: Should we admonish them?

Youth: That won't do any good.

Director: Should we use force?

Youth: Now that's the thing that just might work.

Director: We say to them, "Now, you there! Stop with all your ugliness!" And then we hit them with a stick?

Youth: That might be what they need.

Director: But will they change? Will they be better for the beating that they get?

Youth: No, they won't change.

Director: So what are we to do?

Youth: The most that we can do is try to stop their senseless acts.

Director: We wield our sticks to stop these acts?

Youth: We do.

Director: And what about our friends? Must they wield sticks as well?

Youth: They must.

Director: So far, so good. But now I'm wondering. What happens if some people who are not our friends are much attracted to the power of the sticks. They want to use the sticks, but don't care why.

Youth: You mean they're not deterring ugly acts?

Director: Indeed. In fact, let's say they're ugly in their use of sticks.

Youth: Well, we would have to put a stop to that.

Director: Suppose that there are many more of them than us.

Youth: I think that we're in trouble, then.

Director: Do we put down our sticks?

Youth: How can we? No. We have to fight this new found threat.

Director: And do we just defend ourselves, or do we take the fight to them?

Youth: We take the fight to them, selectively, so we're not overwhelmed.

Director: We are guerrillas in this fight?

Youth: We have to be.

29

Director: Then so it is. But all this talk must have exhausted you, my friend.

Youth: I'm pretty tired, yes.

Director: Then you must rest. But one more thing?

Youth: Of course.

Director: Do you believe your fight, your proper fight, is that of sticks?

Youth: I will not hesitate to fight with sticks, whatever that might mean, if that's what must be done. But no, I think my proper fight lies somewhere else.

Director: What is your proper fight?

Youth: I think I'm meant to fight with words.

Director: Can words be used with force?

Youth: They can.

Director: But does that mean you'll force your words on others, Youth?

Youth: No, I'll be gentle in my use of words — but they will be the truth, and truth has got a force all of its own.

Director: How will you know if you're effective with your words?

Youth: An understanding will be formed.

Director: I see. So have you spoken gentle words of truth to boys at school?

Youth: I've spoken to my friends.

Director: And do you have good understanding with them now?

Youth: It's not as good as I would like.

Director: Why not?

Youth: I wish I knew. But maybe you can help.

Director: But how?

Youth: What if I bring my friends to you?

Director: You want to bring your friends to me? It seems I'll need some help in turn! So, Father, will you lend a hand?

Father: Of course I will.

Director: We'll have to talk to all these friends of Youth and see exactly where the problem lies, what's getting in the way.

Youth: I'm open to the possibility that I might be the problem here. I might not know the truth I think I know, or maybe I don't know the way to speak the truth effectively.

Director: Well, either way, that is the easy case.

Youth: The easy case?

Director: You want to learn. Do you believe your friends all want to learn?

Youth: I don't think that they do.

Director: Can we make someone want to learn, or does he have to want it on his own?

Youth: Can't we encourage him?

Director: That's what we'll do. But if a person really doesn't want to learn we won't have any luck. Don't you agree?

Youth: I do. So if I think a friend has no desire to learn I shouldn't bring him here to meet with us?

Father: Perhaps he really wants to learn but it's not obvious to you.

Youth: Then I'll bring all my friends?

Father: Why not? We'll throw a party for the truth!

Youth: But that's the thing. What do I tell them we'll be doing here?

Director: Why not just tell them that we'll read a book together, Youth?

Youth: You mean aloud?

Director: Why not?

Youth: What sort of book?

Director: A book that touches on philosophy, what else?

Youth: You think they'd come for that?

Director: The ones who would will likely be the ones we want. Or wouldn't you agree?

Youth: You have a point. And so we read? That's it?

Director: We read and talk about the things we read.

Father: I like this way. A point raised in the book can spur us on to talk about a point we take from life, a point that's parallel to what we've read. And so our conversation on the truth of things arises naturally.

Youth: I think this just might work.

Father: I think it's worth a try. And if it doesn't work, so what? We stop and try to think up something else.

Youth: I'd like to thank you both.

Director: For what?

Youth: For this.

Director: No need to thank us, Youth.

Youth: But there is something more. I want to thank you both for speaking to me like a man, and not a boy.

Director: Then we owe thanks to you, as well.

Youth: For what?

Director: For listening and speaking truth to us.

Youth: I'll always listen and speak truth to you. I know that you will do the same.

Director: Then we're well matched as friends.

Youth: You know, you are a different sort of friend than those I have at school.

Director: Because I am your father's friend?

Youth: No, it's because you're serious about the truth.

Director: Do you believe I'm tragically inclined?

Youth: Why, no. You're serious and light at once. I think that is your strength.

Director: But if I had to choose, which way do you believe I'd go?

Youth: Director, I don't think you'll ever have to choose.

Director: But why?

Youth: Your friends won't let you. I, at any rate, will not.

Director: Then you would be my guardian?

Youth: That's right. I'll help to guard your strength.

Director: Then I will try to guard your strength in turn. But now it's time for me to go. Good night, my friends.

Youth: Good night.